Contents

RY –
36

List of tables

List of figures

List of boxes

Acronyms and abbreviations

DAC   Development Assistance Committee (of the OECD)

FDI   foreign direct investment

G7   the seven most powerful industrial nations (USA, UK, Germany, Japan, Italy, France, and Canada)

G8   G7 + Russia

GDP   gross domestic product

GNI   gross national income

GNP   gross national product

HIPC   Highly Indebted Poor Country

IDA   International Development Association

IFF   International Finance Facility

IMF   International Monetary Fund

MDG   Millennium Development Goal

OA   Official Aid

ODA   Official Development Assistance

OECD   Organisation for Economic Co-operation and Development

PRSC   Poverty Reduction Support Credit

PRGF   Poverty Reduction and Growth Facility

PRSP   Poverty Reduction Strategy Paper

PSIA   Poverty and Social Impact Analysis

Summary

'We are the first generation that can look extreme poverty in the eye, and say this and mean it –
we have the cash, we have the drugs, we have the science. Do we have the will to make poverty
history?'
Bono, September 2004

In 2005, the leaders of rich countries have the opportunity to lift millions of people out of
poverty. At the G8 Summit, at the UN Special Session on the Millennium Development Goals
(MDGs), and at a ministerial conference of the World Trade Organisation (WTO), trade rules,
aid, and the unsustainable debt of developing countries – issues critical to the future of the
world's poorest people – will be up for discussion. But will world leaders deliver on their
rhetoric? In 2000, rich countries made a commitment to play their part in ensuring that the
MDGs are met – but their promises remain unfulfilled. Five years later, they should ensure
that a new round of international summitry becomes a platform for action.

The Millennium Development Goals, chosen on the grounds that they were realistic and
achievable, are a commitment by global leaders to halve poverty and hunger, provide education
for all, improve standards of health, halt the spread of major diseases such as HIV/AIDS,
and slow down environmental degradation by 2015.

A vital aim of these goals is that the poorest countries will have the finance needed to achieve
them. To do this, rich countries have promised to provide a very small fraction of their wealth –
just 0.7 per cent of their national income – and to improve the way in which they give aid,
to make it work best for poverty reduction, and to end the burden of debt which means that
low-income countries must pay out $100 million every day to their creditors. For rich-country
donors, making this finance available is not simply an act of charity: it is both a moral
obligation and a matter of justice – born of a collective duty to guarantee the rights of all
citizens, and the responsibility of rich countries to recognise their role in creating the debt
crisis which continues to threaten the prospects of poor countries. A failure to meet these
obligations also has consequences for rich countries themselves, with global poverty
threatening the prosperity and security of the entire international community.

Time for action to meet the MDGs is running out, yet progress has been unforgivably slow.
Only one goal – halving income poverty – has any chance of being met, but even this is due to

progress in just a handful of countries. The first target – enrolling all girls in primary and secondary school by 2005 – is certain to be missed. The poorest people will pay the price for this failure. If the world fails to act to meet even these minimal goals, and current trends are allowed to continue,

- 45 million more children will die between now and 2015
- 247 million more people in sub-Saharan Africa will be living on less than $1 a day in 2015
- 97 million more children will still be out of school in 2015
- 53 million more people in the world will lack proper sanitation facilities.

Tackling global poverty requires more than money: poor countries' prospects are also undermined by unfair trade rules, the violent consequences of the arms trade, and the impacts of global warming. Poor-country governments must also fulfil their commitments to fight poverty. But, without finance, these countries will not be able to take advantage of global trade and investment opportunities, or protect their citizens' basic rights to life, good health, and education.

Rich countries today give half as much, as a proportion of their income, as they did in the 1960s.

The sums that rich countries invest in global poverty reduction are shamefully small. At an average of $80 per person per year in rich countries, the sum is equivalent to the price of a weekly cup of coffee. What is more, the wealthier these countries have become, the less they have given in aid. Rich countries today give half as much, as a proportion of their income, as they did in the 1960s. In 1960–65, rich countries spent on average 0.48 per cent of their combined national incomes on aid. By 1980–85 they were spending just 0.34 per cent. By 2003, the average had dropped as low as 0.24 per cent.

It is no surprise that vital poverty-reduction programmes are failing for lack of finance. Cambodia and Tanzania are among the poorest countries in the world, yet they require at least double the level of external financing that they currently receive if they are to achieve their poverty-reduction targets. Global initiatives to support poor countries to achieve universal education and combat HIV/AIDS are starved of cash. Despite the fact that HIV infection rates are rising in sub-Saharan Africa, the Global Fund to Fight AIDS, TB, and Malaria is assured of only one quarter of the funds that it needs for 2005. And poor countries continue to pay out more to their creditors than they spend on essential public services. Low-income countries paid $39 billion to service their debts in 2003, while they received only $27 billion in aid. As a result, countries such as Zambia spend more on debt servicing than they spend on education.

The price is small

Meeting the UN target of allocating just 0.7 per cent of national income to aid – a target set in 1970 – would generate $120 billion, enough to meet the MDGs and other vital poverty-reduction goals. But only five of the 22 major donors – none of them from the seven most powerful nations (the G7) – are meeting that target. In the last year, the UK and Spain have set themselves firm timetables to reach the target of 0.7. But 12 donors still have no timetable to get there, and many appear to be in no hurry: on current trends in spending, Canada will not reach the target until 2025, the USA will not reach it until 2040, and Germany will not get there before 2087.

Rich countries can easily afford to deliver the necessary aid and debt relief. For rich countries, spending 0.7 per cent of their national income on aid is equal to a mere one-fifth of their expenditure on defence and one half of their expenditure on domestic farm subsidies. The USA (at just 0.14 per cent, the least generous donor in terms of aid as a proportion of its national income) is spending more than twice as much on the war in Iraq as it would cost to increase its aid budget to 0.7 per cent, and six times more on its military programme.

Nor is 0.7 per cent very great when compared with the priorities of global consumers, who spend $33 billion each year on cosmetics and perfume – significantly more than the $20–25 billion required for Africa to meet the MDG targets.

Cancelling the debts of 32 of the poorest countries would also be small change for the rich nations. The cost to the richest countries would amount to $1.8 billion each year over the next ten years – or on average a mere $2.10 for each of their citizens every year. If Italy and the USA were to pay their fair shares, it would cost each of their citizens $1.20 per year. Meanwhile, the IMF holds the third-largest gold reserve in the world – a reserve that is neither needed nor used in full. Revaluation or sale of the gold could raise more than $30 billion – more than would be needed to cancel the remaining debts to the IMF and World Bank of all the countries eligible for relief under the Highly Indebted Poor Countries initiative.

Aid works ...

And aid works. Millions of children are in school in Tanzania, Uganda, Kenya, Malawi, and Zambia, thanks to money provided by debt relief and aid. For the same reason, Ugandans no longer have to pay for basic health care, a policy which resulted in an increase of 50 to 100 per cent in attendance at Ugandan health clinics and doubled the rate of immunisations. Roads built with foreign aid mean that Ethiopian farmers have the potential to reach local and international markets to sell their crops more easily, while children in rural areas can travel to schools more easily, and people can reach hospitals more quickly – which is often a critical factor affecting maternal and infant mortality rates. In Bolivia, financial support to indigenous peoples has amplified their political voice – in particular when it supports women's groups to monitor local government's implementation of policies to promote equality for women and men. Key demands such as protection against sexual violence and improved standards of reproductive-health care have now been included in local-government plans.

History also shows that aid has been vital in eradicating global diseases. From the late 1960s, more than $100 million was targeted to eradicate smallpox – a feat achieved worldwide by 1980.

And aid has been essential in rebuilding countries shattered by war. In Mozambique, financial support from UN agencies, bilateral donors, and NGOs facilitated a process of national reconciliation, peacefully repatriating nearly two million refugees, disarming 96,000 former soldiers, and clearing landmines.

Countries now considered 'developed' would not enjoy their current standards of living if it had not been for aid. After World War II, 16 western European nations benefited from grants from the USA worth more than $75 billion in today's terms – grants which underpinned their economic recovery and hence created today's peace and prosperity. US aid also financed mass education and imports of essential goods to South Korea and Taiwan, laying the foundations for their rapid future growth, while European Union Structural Funds have supported growth in Spain and other southern European countries.

But today's poorest countries – even those where it has been shown that aid can be used productively – have yet to see the necessary aid extended to them. Meanwhile, marginalised from the global economy, their access to other forms of external finance is limited. For the foreseeable future, aid will and should be the means to offset the lack of finance available for the poorest countries and communities. Aid also has intrinsic advantages: if managed well, it can be targeted to those communities that need it most, in a stable and predictable manner conducive to long-term investments in health care, education, clean water, sanitation, and other essential infrastructure.

… and it could work even better

Almost 30 per cent of G7 aid money is tied to an obligation to buy goods and services from the donor country.

However, rich-country donors need to make aid work better if poverty is to be significantly reduced. Increases in aid budgets can and must go hand-in-hand with improvements in the way that aid is delivered.

When aid-giving becomes politicised, poor people lose out – but many donors' priorities are still determined by their own strategic interests. Two top recipients of French aid – French Polynesia and New Caledonia – and one top recipient of US aid – Israel – are high-income countries. The 'war on terror' threatens to divert aid away from those who need it most. Aid is again being used as a political tool, with one-third of the increase in aid in 2002 resulting from large allocations to Afghanistan and Pakistan. And the goals of development aid are being redefined to suit the new security agenda: in Denmark, Japan, and Australia, 'combating terrorism' is now an explicit aim of official aid programmes.

Too often domestic interests take precedence: almost 30 per cent of G7 aid money is tied to an obligation to buy goods and services from the donor country. The practice is not only self-serving, but highly inefficient; yet it is employed widely by Italy and the USA. Despite donors' agreements to untie aid to the poorest countries, only six of the 22 major donor countries have almost or completely done so.

The management burden and uncertainty of aid delivery that many donors create weakens the effectiveness of the governments that they aim to support. In Tanzania in 2002–03, the government received 275 donor missions, 123 from the World Bank alone, demanding time-consuming attention by scarce skilled personnel. An Oxfam survey of donor practices across 11 developing countries in 2004 found as follows.

- In 52 per cent of reported cases, donors' procedures mean that government officials spend 'too much' or 'excessive' amounts of time in reporting to donors. The World Bank and the USA were named as the worst donors according to this criterion.

- Developing-country governments should expect delays. Only in one in three cases does aid arrive on time – and the European Commission is rated the worst offender, with one-fifth of its aid arriving more than one year late.

- Aid may be here today, but it could be gone tomorrow. In 70 per cent of cases, donors commit aid for three years or less – even though, in order to guarantee a complete primary education for one generation of children, funding would be needed for six years.

An Oxfam survey of six major donors found that only in one in three cases does aid arrive on time.

The administrative problem is compounded when donors attach large numbers of detailed conditions to their funding. Oxfam's analysis of World Bank loan conditions, for instance, found that the Bank requires governments of countries such as Ethiopia to carry out approximately 80 policy changes per year. Tanzania's donors between them dictate that the country should carry out 78 policy reforms in one year. This practice undermines countries' ability to choose their own reform paths, meaning that aid money is less likely to support sustainable reforms, adapted to suit local circumstances. Such conditions are rarely based on independent assessments of their impact on people living in poverty. In Malawi, for example, where donors commissioned an analysis concerning the privatisation of the state agricultural marketing board at the very moment of a national food crisis, the results were withheld for two years. Then, despite the study's recommendations to delay privatisation until the regulations necessary to protect the poorest were in place, it was ignored in the conditions attached to new World Bank loans.

Rich-country and multilateral donors have committed themselves to change their practices. In 2003 they signed the Rome Declaration: a clear statement of intent to reform the delivery of aid. Some are making progress, mostly by collaborating to deliver joint funds directly to sector ministries or government treasuries; but others lag behind, as demonstrated by the Oxfam survey. While donors are quick to hold governments to account for their use of aid, there is as yet very little done to hold donors to account for their management of aid. Initiatives such as independent monitoring or recipient-government reviews of donor practice occur largely on an *ad hoc* and voluntary basis.

Ensuring that Southern governments deliver development

Developing countries, as well as donors, have a responsibility to meet the MDGs. And well-functioning and poverty-focused governments can of course make the best use of aid. This means combating corruption, building strong and accountable public sectors which have the necessary staff to deliver vital services, and ensuring that parliaments, civil society, and the media can monitor public spending and act as watchdogs against corruption.

There has been substantial progress in the performance and accountability of many poor-country governments. Democracy is taking root in sub-Saharan Africa, for instance, with elections held in 44 out of 50 countries in the past decade, while independent TV and radio stations are being established across the continent. And civil-society groups are increasingly calling governments to account: in Malawi, education groups now check whether schools receive the textbooks and chalk promised to them in the government budget, and they report their findings in the media and in parliament.

But obviously in many countries there is a long way to go: developing-country governments, for instance, must increase the amount of money devoted to basic social services, in line with a UN recommendation to spend at least 20 per cent on these sectors. The practice of charging user fees for basic education and health services should be abolished.

Donors can play their part in furthering these developments. This includes not ignoring corruption, but tackling it by investing in a strong and efficient public sector and removing the global incentives – tax havens and weak regulation – that allow corruption to flourish. Creating donor-led structures outside governments, or avoiding certain countries altogether, can be counter-productive – merely serving to weaken them further. And such strategies risk diverting money away from those in the global community who need it most.

In 2005, Oxfam will form part of the 'Global Call for Action Against Poverty' coalition, aiming to make poverty history. The call unites a huge range of groups from South and North, including national and regional civil-society networks, trade unions, faith communities, and international organisations. It is a chance for millions of people to tell world leaders that poverty is an injustice that is not inevitable.

This report is part of Oxfam's call to action in 2005. In it, Oxfam's key recommendations in relation to aid and debt are as follows:

All donor members of the OECD's Development Assistance Committee (DAC) should adopt the following measures.

Increase finance for poverty reduction:

- Cancel 100 per cent of the debt of the poorest countries where relief is needed to enable them to reach the MDGs: both bilateral debt, and the debts owed to the World Bank and African Development Bank.

- Provide at least $50 billion in aid immediately, in addition to existing aid budgets, and set binding timetables in 2005 to ensure that the 0.7 per cent target is met in all donor countries by 2010.

- In addition to giving 0.7 per cent of national income as aid, support innovative mechanisms such as the International Finance Facility (IFF) and international taxation to ensure immediate and sustainable development financing.

Make aid work best for poverty reduction:

- Fully implement Rome Declaration commitments to improve the delivery of aid and completely untie aid, including types of assistance omitted from DAC recommendations, namely food aid and Technical Assistance.

- Restrict the use of conditions to requirements for financial accountability and broadly agreed goals on poverty reduction and gender equity.

The World Bank and IMF should take the following actions.

- Cancel 100 per cent of the debts owed to them by the poorest countries where relief is needed to enable them to reach the MDGs; finance this measure by revaluing IMF gold reserves and using the resources thus generated.

- Restrict the use of conditions to requirements for financial accountability measures and broadly agreed goals on poverty reduction and gender equity.

Developing-country governments should take the following measures.

- Demonstrate their commitment to poverty reduction by meeting the UN recommendation to spend 20 per cent of public budgets on basic social services, and transparently directing the money to benefit poor people.

- Institutionalise, through legislation if necessary, parliamentary and civil-society participation in the making and implementation of policies that will benefit poor people, also guaranteeing civil and political rights to free and fair elections, freedom of expression, and the rule of law.

Introduction

'We will spare no effort to free our fellow men, women and children from the abject and dehumanising conditions of extreme poverty...we are committed to making the right to development a reality for everyone and to freeing the entire human race from want.'
UN Millennium Declaration, 2000

'These days, if you are without money, they leave you to die. If my children are ill, and I have money from selling sisal and firewood, I take them to the nearest town. If there's no money, I use herbs ... if God takes them, we have done our best.'
Amekwi Lokana, mother of six, Kenya, 2002

In 2000, the leaders and heads of state of 189 countries signed the Millennium Declaration, which set a series of targets for global action against poverty by 2015. Meeting the goals, known as the Millennium Development Goals (MDGs), will not end poverty, but it could nevertheless make a positive difference to millions of people.[1] However, at current rates of progress, even these intermediate targets are unlikely to be met. Only the target of halving income poverty has any chance of being met, but even this is due to progress in a mere handful of countries: many regions, including Africa, will not achieve it.[2] The target of achieving gender equity in primary and secondary education by 2005 is certain to be missed.

Table 1: The Millennium Development Goals (MDGs)

Goal	① Eradicate income poverty and hunger	② Achieve universal primary education	③ Promote gender equality and empower women	④ Reduce child mortality	⑤ Improve maternal health	⑥ Combat HIV/AIDS, malaria and other diseases	⑦ Ensure environmental sustainability	⑧ Develop a global partnership for development
Key targets	Halve the proportion of people living on less than $1 a day by 2015. Halve the proportion of people who suffer from hunger by 2015	Ensure that all children complete a full course of primary schooling by 2015	Eliminate gender disparity in primary and secondary education by 2005, and in all levels of education by 2015	Reduce the mortality rate of children under five by two-thirds by 2015	Reduce by three-quarters the ratio of women dying in childbirth by 2015	Halt and begin to reverse the incidence of HIV/AIDS and other major diseases by 2015	Halve by 2015 the proportion of people without access to safe drinking water and basic sanitation	Develop a non-discriminatory and rules-based trading system, provide more generous aid and deal comprehensively with the debt problem

Providing the aid and debt relief needed by the world's poorest countries was one of the key promises made by rich nations in their commitment to the MDGs, expressed in Goal 8. The time to act is running out. If the spread of HIV/AIDS is to be contained, intervention must happen now, because 14,000 new cases of infection are occurring every day.[3] If large numbers of children are not to be orphaned by the HIV/AIDS crisis, treatment needs to be available for their parents as soon as possible. If all children are to complete primary school in 2015, millions more need to be in classes within the next five years. If gaps between girls and boys at all levels of education are to be eradicated by 2015, then millions of girls need to be starting school this year.

Global poverty threatens our shared prosperity and security.

In the twenty-first century, the price of not investing in sustainable development for poor communities will be felt not only in developing countries, but across the world. Global poverty threatens our shared prosperity and security. Environmental crises and natural disasters, diseases, and drug trafficking know no national borders.[4] Poverty heightens the likelihood of conflict and unrest: the risk of civil war is much higher in low-income countries.[5] New threats to the peace and security of rich nations arise from poverty and gross inequality. Criminal and terrorist networks are more likely to operate where state institutions are weak. And the actions of rich nations do not go un-noted by the rest of the world, which perceives that the rich powers intervene militarily when their own security is threatened, but rarely invest in long-term development in accordance with their obligations to ensure the security of rights for all.

Of course, giving more aid is far from being the only international action needed to end poverty. Many poor countries are undermined by global trade rules that are rigged against their interests; they are exposed to the violent consequences of the arms trade; and they bear the brunt of the most severe impacts of global warming. The value of aid itself is diminished by other rich-country policies – by the costs to poor countries of Northern tariff barriers, for instance, or unnecessarily high prices charged for patented medicines. Tackling these problems calls for far more than development finance. But, without aid, the poorest countries will not be able to take advantage of the opportunities that exist for trade and investment, or defend their interests in the international arena – let alone protect their citizens' basic rights.

This report argues that more and better development aid is necessary in order to fight an effective war on poverty. Although humanitarian aid in emergencies is also vital, it is not the main focus of this report. Unless otherwise stated, the word 'aid' is used here to refer to both aid and debt relief – the costs of which are currently included in donors' aid budgets. Part 1 argues that aid works, and that rich countries have a duty and responsibility to give it. Part 2 sets out the human cost of donors' broken promises to deliver aid – and demonstrates how easily they could afford it. Part 3 shows that donors still need to make aid work better for poverty reduction. Part 4 explains how developing-country governments must make aid a more effective tool for poverty reduction.

1
The argument
for aid

Tanzania: a new classroom at Mapinduzi primary school in Shinyanga town.

1
The argument for aid

'When I was nine my father died. That's when my problems started. My mother didn't have any money to pay for my school fees, and the teachers used to send me home from school. But now I'm happy....school fees have been abolished, and no one is stopping me coming to school.'
Winifred Kiyabo, Asunda village school, Tanzania, 2002

When the government of Tanzania made primary education free and compulsory in 2002, an extra 1.6 million children started attending school. The policy would not have been possible without the international debt relief that enabled the government to waive school fees, and could not have been sustained without the support from donors that has financed the construction of new schools and classrooms.

Thanks to development aid, Tanzanian children are not alone in obtaining their fundamental right to education.[6] Donors' support for primary education in Ethiopia has facilitated the entry of four million more children into school over the last five years.[7] In Uganda, Malawi, Kenya, and Zambia, too, fees for primary education have now been abolished, thanks in large part to external finance.

Winifred and other schoolchildren across Africa are living proof that aid can and does give people the opportunity to progress out of poverty. Of course, not all aid has delivered such significant results – and high-profile cases of misused and mismanaged aid tend to tarnish the reputation of all development finance. But there is plenty of evidence to demonstrate that aid does work. However, far more of it is needed. For every child in school, millions of others are still deprived of their basic rights for lack of funding.

Delivering justice, not charity

For rich countries, providing aid to help to end global poverty is an obligation and a matter of justice, not an act of charity. At the UN General Assembly in 2000, the world's heads of state and governments recognised their *'collective responsibility to uphold the principles of human dignity, equality and equity at the global level'*[8] and committed themselves to developing a global compact for development, of which the provision of aid by rich countries is a part.

In failing to live up to this responsibility, rich-country donors neglect their duty to guarantee the rights of all citizens, as expressed in the UN Declaration of Human Rights:

'everyone has the right to a standard of living adequate for the health and well-being of himself and of his family, including food, clothing, housing and medical care' (UN 1948), and in the 1986 Declaration on the Right to Development: *'every human person and all peoples are entitled to participate in, contribute to and enjoy social, cultural and political development.'*[9]

Rich countries also deny equality of opportunity to billions of people. They perpetuate a *status quo* characterised by intolerable inequality: today, the average income in the richest twenty countries in the world is 37 times that in the poorest twenty.[10] In upholding such an unequal global system, they sanction a fundamental injustice.

The average income in the richest twenty countries in the world is 37 times that in the poorest twenty.

And in failing to cancel the debts of poor-country nations to rich-country creditors, rich countries commit an even more express act of injustice. Creditors fostered irresponsible lending to developing-country regimes and encouraged the accumulation of new loans to finance structural adjustment policies which did little to improve, and may have even worsened, the economic situation of borrower nations.[11] Too often the current generation is paying for past debts accumulated in an 'odious' fashion – by leaders who accumulated debts without the consent of their populations and did not use the money in their interests, all of which was known by creditors at the time. The failure to deal comprehensively with the debt crisis means that poor nations now face a situation in which they will pay more back through protracted debt-service arrangements than they originally borrowed.[12] And they continue to be caught in a vicious cycle, paying out more in debt servicing than they receive in aid. Low-income countries spent $39 billion on servicing their debts in 2003, and received $27 billion in aid.[13]

Aid works

Aid is used to reduce poverty in many ways: by stimulating economic growth, by increasing government revenue for funding basic services, and by enabling poor communities to engage in political processes. Such diverse interventions, typically made in complex policy environments, create obvious difficulties when drawing broad conclusions about the effectiveness of aid. But there are many clear examples of cases in which international aid has had dramatic impacts on levels of poverty.

Kick-starting growth

When the US Secretary of State George Marshall announced his post-war rescue plan for Europe in 1947, he initiated an act of financial largesse by the USA that it has never repeated.[14] For the 16 western European nations that received the equivalent of at least US$75 billion at today's prices – mostly in the form of grants – the 'Marshall Plan' was heralded as a 'lifeline to sinking men',[15] a measure which provided a 'critical margin' of support to underpin their economic recovery. Likewise, US aid to South Korea and Taiwan financed mass education and imports of essential goods, and supported land reform, laying the foundations for future growth

Ssarah Errington/Oxfam

Ghana: vaccination clinic at Kubori Health Centre

which transformed these countries from nations as poor as most African states in 1960 into middle-income aid donors themselves today.[16] More recently, European Union aid has buttressed economic growth in southern European countries: in Spain, Structural Funds from the late 1980s are credited with supporting growth and helping to avoid greater economic decline during the economic crisis of the mid-1990s.[17]

Tackling global diseases

International finance has been key to the global eradication of disease. From the late 1960s, more than $100 million in aid was targeted to the worldwide eradication of smallpox– a feat achieved by 1980. In 1974, donor governments and companies collaborated to eliminate river blindness, a disease causing loss of sight and disfigurement, from 11 countries in West Africa. In the 1970s, UNICEF and the World Health Organization launched a major child-immunisation programme which ensured that immunisation rates had doubled and even trebled in many countries by the mid-1980s.[18]

Facilitating post-conflict reconstruction

Support from UN agencies, bilateral donors, and NGOs was critical to Mozambique's post-war reconstruction in the 1990s. Donor aid – initially exceeding 80 per cent of the government budget – helped to pay for monitoring of the peace accords and facilitated a process of national reconciliation. It was critical to repatriating nearly two million refugees, disarming and reintegrating 96,000 former soldiers from both sides, helping to pay election expenses, and clearing landmines.[19]

Turning debt into development

Where debt relief has been delivered, there have been real gains for people living in poverty. In countries that have qualified for the Highly Indebted Poor Countries (HIPC) initiative, which aims to relieve the debt burden of 42 of the most indebted poor countries, spending on health and education, especially on rural clinics and primary schools, has risen. And because debt relief is stable, long-term, and channelled to government budgets, it is spent on vital recurrent costs, such as salaries for teachers and health workers. In Mali, more than 5,000 community teachers are given a monthly stipend, provided out of HIPC relief. In Benin, more than half of HIPC relief has been used to recruit staff for rural health clinics, combat HIV/AIDS, promote anti-malaria and immunisation programmes, and improve access to safe water.[20]

Building essential infrastructure

Weak infrastructure – in health, education, and transport services – creates systematic barriers to development. It can impede developing countries from taking advantage of international export opportunities: transport costs in sub-Saharan Africa add around 30 per cent to the price of exports, due to poor roads and port facilities.[21] (See Box 1.)

Empowering the most marginalised communities

Aid can also play a vital role in promoting democracy and a more equitable society, by increasing the demand for political accountability, as formerly marginalised communities are supported to organise and participate in the decision-making processes which affect their lives. (See Box 2.)

Aid is a critical source of finance for the poorest countries

The world's poorest countries are those with the most limited financing options. With low national incomes, they have less capacity to tax and save.[22] Excluded from the global economy, they find that their access to other forms of external finance (export earnings, foreign direct investment [FDI], and other forms of private capital and remittances) is restricted. This makes aid an essential mechanism for redistributing resources to the most economically marginalised countries and communities. Managed well, it can do so quickly and directly.

Overall, the volume of private flows exceeds the volume of aid and hence is of great importance for developing countries. Globally, FDI and remittances are the two largest sources of external finance for developing countries, and capital market flows to developing countries have been increasing in volume. But they are often concentrated in a few, large countries: in 2003, just 10 countries received 69 per cent of all foreign direct investment to the developing world, while a mere five issued 60 per cent of all developing-country bonds, one type of asset traded on financial markets.[23]

Box 1: Improving road access in Ethiopia

'In Ethiopia, to reach a road from any place takes an average of six hours…how can you then expect people to be productive?'
Bekele Negussie, Planning and Programming Manager, Ethiopian Roads Authority

Women sell far more sugar cane beside the Addis–Djibouti highway since it was upgraded.

In Ethiopia, good roads are critical if people are to reach schools and health clinics easily (an important factor in improving child and maternal mortality rates).* They are vital too in reducing the time and cost to farmers when taking their crops to market – an especially important benefit, given that 85 per cent of the population live in rural areas, working mostly as small-scale farmers. Moreover, because Ethiopia is land-locked, better road networks are vital to improving trade links and therefore increasing export revenue.

Foreign aid has played a crucial role in improving road travel and transport in Ethiopia. External donors have financed around 40 per cent of the government's road-development programme to date, resulting in a 40 per cent increase in the national road network.**

With good roads, it also becomes easier to bring services to the local community: *'There is a lot of evidence to suggest that teachers are not willing to go where there is no road'*, says Bekele Negussie. *'If there is access, agricultural agents, teachers, health workers, they can all go in.'* People living along the new highway report greater frequency of minibuses to take them to nearby towns, making it easier to sell their produce and visit families and friends. *'Two years ago there were two buses a day; now there are 20'*, reports Hosseana Hailemariam, working for Oxfam in Deder, close to a new road. *'The buses are also cheaper, and people no longer have to stay overnight in the cities, which reduces their overall costs.'*

Phase Two of the programme will focus on improving infrastructure in the villages, aiming to reduce the time taken by women and girls to collect water and fuel, by improving roads, footpaths, bridges, and wells.

* Recent studies have shown that better road networks have an important role to play in improving child health, by reducing the time taken to access clinics and hospitals (Leipziger et el. 2003).

** So far the Road Development Programme, launched in 1997, has focused on the upgrading and rehabilitation of existing roads, such as the main highway from Addis Ababa to neighbouring Djibouti, now provided with an all-weather surface for the first time. The government has deliberately opted to employ large numbers of labourers rather than import machinery for road construction, on the grounds that not only is it less expensive, but it will also provide an injection of cash for the community and encourage local ownership of the roads.

(Source: Fraser for Oxfam GB, 2004a)

Box 2: Amplifying the voice of indigenous peoples in Bolivia

'*When we women are united, organised, and know what we want, we can get our demands addressed and make our dreams a possibility.*'
Rosmery Irusta De Bellot, Local Community Leader for Urban Development, Bolivia

In Bolivia, a lack of political influence has historically played a part in the exclusion and poverty of the largely rural indigenous peoples. Constituting 60 per cent of the population, such communities have benefited from aid that is intended to make local government policies more responsive to the needs of poor communities, and to build up the capacity of indigenous people to participate in political processes.

Since 1994, when the 'Law of Popular Participation' passed responsibility for 20 per cent of central revenue to local councils, poverty-focused debt-relief programmes, such as the HIPC initiative, have released more central funds to be channelled to local government assemblies, helping to redress the previous bias in favour of urban communities.

As a result, indigenous representatives and women have been elected to serve in local government for the first time, some as mayors. Further aid has enabled these groups to take advantage of legal reforms granting indigenous rights to title, management, and control of resources. Substantial compensation has been won from multinational companies for damage done during their operations in indigenous areas.

Women have been empowered to gain a fairer share of resources and better service provision. In Cochabamba, women's groups such as IFFI (Women's Integrated Training Institute) are supported by, among others, Novib (Oxfam Netherlands) and Oxfam GB to monitor municipal government, verifying compliance and transparency in the implementation of public policies which promote gender equality. '*We have managed to get our gender demands included in the Municipal Development Plan in concrete ways: protection against sexual and domestic violence, improved reproductive-health care and training, and access to credit and education*', says Felicidad Bilbao Hidalgo, a neighbourhood association leader.

(Source: Whiston for Oxfam GB, 2004 forthcoming)

Peru: a street demonstration by the Women's Organisation of Santo Domingo

Annie Bungeroth/Oxfam

Figure 1: The poorest countries attract little global finance

Sub-Saharan Africa's percentage share of external financing (except aid flows) to all developing countries, 2002

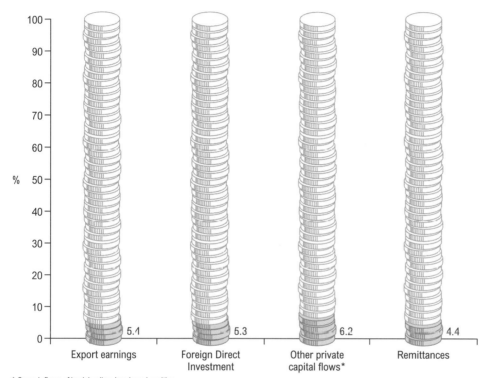

* Gross inflows of bank lending, bonds and equities

(Sources: Oxfam, using data from World Development Indicators and Global Development Finance)

For the poorest nations, private investment is not at present an option. Armed conflict, poor infrastructure, and the lack of a skilled workforce makes them unattractive to private capital, and unable to borrow on commercial markets. Despite the promise of increases in other resources, it is unlikely in sheer volume terms that such increases could provide the finance for poverty reduction in these countries at the pace so urgently necessary in the foreseeable future – especially for countries with small markets and difficult geographical conditions. But aid flows can be deliberately used to offset these limitations.

The experience of Africa proves the point. In 2002, sub-Saharan Africa, home to around 10 per cent of the world's population, captured only around five per cent of financial flows other than aid[24] (see Figure 1).

Figure 2: Aid is second only to export earnings in importance

External finance to sub-Saharan Africa as a percentage of national income (GDP), 2002

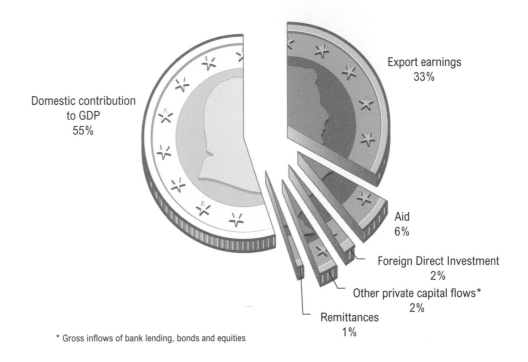

Domestic contribution
to GDP
55%

Export earnings
33%

Aid
6%

Foreign Direct Investment
2%

Other private capital flows*
2%

Remittances
1%

* Gross inflows of bank lending, bonds and equities

(Sources: Oxfam, using data from World Development Indicators, Global Development Finance, and OECD Development Assistance Committee)

As a result, the economic impact of aid is already significant: in sub-Saharan Africa, aid flows are second in importance only to export earnings (see Figure 2).

Not only is aid virtually the only realistic financial option for the poorest countries in the foreseeable future, but it can have a greater impact on reducing poverty than other forms of finance. It can be deliberately and quickly targeted to reduce poverty, and directed to those countries and communities with the greatest need of external assistance. Although other flows can be beneficial, trade and private capital flows rely on a more indirect route of improving growth to raise incomes. And whereas private remittances are spent by households, aid can support the public provision of important services. These functions of aid are critical to redressing both national and global inequalities, and to addressing the growing disparities between rich and poor groups.

Aid can be a more stable source of national income. Poor countries dependent on exports of primary commodities are exposed to price fluctuations, whereas there is evidence that private financial flows (especially non-FDI flows) are even more volatile than aid flows.[25] Further, aid finances important things that do not attract market-oriented finance: global public goods such as environmental protection, humanitarian assistance, and disaster protection.[26]

Aid pessimism needs reassessment

Despite the evident value of so much development finance, 'aid pessimism' has often prevailed in policy circles and public opinion. Such pessimism is not unfounded, and Parts 3 and 4 of this report present ways in which both donors and recipient governments could and must do more to make aid work best for poverty reduction. Aid pessimists have used findings from academic reviews of the past effectiveness of aid to justify their arguments – and to justify reductions in rich-country aid budgets. But the basis for these arguments needs careful scrutiny.

Reassessment of this academic literature is necessary on three counts. First, many surveys have focused on investigating the link between aid and growth, to the detriment of other means of poverty reduction, such as spending on basic services, and without much attention to the fact that growth may not inherently lead to poverty reduction. Second, recent revisions of the literature, such as those undertaken by Hansen and Tarp, have found that of all the studies ever undertaken to investigate the relationship between aid and growth, those with negative results are in the minority.[27] Third, re-evaluating some of the older pessimistic research with new techniques has reversed the conclusions, demonstrating in fact a positive relationship between aid and growth.[28]

Other critiques of aid – such as those undertaken by Dollar and Pritchett and Burnside and Dollar for the World Bank – stress that it works only in certain domestic policy environments.[29] Of course, well-functioning and poverty-focused governments can make best use of aid – as Part 4 of this report testifies. But not only can aid be used productively in other contexts, it would be wrong to restrict its use only to those countries judged 'ideal' on highly subjective criteria – defined in these studies as low budget deficits, low inflation, openness to external trade, and a diffuse measure of 'institutional quality'.[30] Further, the research results underlying these conclusions are very sensitive to changes in the assumptions made.[31] And they fail to account for the diverse types of aid provided, such as food aid and emergency aid, whose primary aims are humanitarian relief, not economic growth. They also overlook the environment into which aid is delivered (post-conflict countries or those undergoing negative external shocks may be better able than other countries to use larger amounts of aid, for instance[32]). They disregard too any possible impacts of the manner of its delivery: it may be that the uncertainty of aid flows is more strongly related to poor growth than to the policy environment, for example.[33] And, as Parts 3 and 4 of this report argue, on-going reforms in the delivery and use of aid can make a significant difference. Past performance is not necessarily a guide for the future.

There are concerns about the macro-economic effect of introducing large volumes of aid into an economy; these concerns refer to the phenomenon (known as 'the Dutch disease') whereby inflows of foreign currency cause inflation and damage export competitiveness. But the debate is highly contested. The effects can be mitigated to a large degree by prudent economic management; and the fact is that many developing countries are currently experiencing low rates of inflation, which provide a sound basis for greater aid flows.

More salient than the results of historical studies of aid effectiveness is the present concern that poor countries will simply not be able to spend increased amounts of aid, because they lack 'absorption capacity' – the personnel and institutions to deliver the benefits to the intended recipients. But donors and governments can invest in improving this capacity. As Parts 3 and 4 of this report explain, donors often make such problems worse by their reluctance to invest in recurrent expenditures such as salaries (traditionally preferring to concentrate on physical infrastructure, such as classrooms) or meaningful staff training. Imposing cumbersome procedures on recipient countries and delivering aid flows in a highly unpredictable fashion also delay the flow of aid and undermine a government's ability to invest for the long term in its institutions. And aid can be adapted to particular circumstances, with flows phased according to need.

Recent analysis also challenges pessimism about the effectiveness of aid. A recent study by the World Bank concludes that in 18 low-income countries more aid could be used productively over the next decade. The study estimates that sub-Saharan African countries in the sample can use a supplementary increase in aid of about 60 per cent in the medium term.[34]

2

Small change:
the costs of aid

Kenya: A break between classes at Mashimoni Squatters primary school, Kibera

2
Small change: the costs of aid

'We believe that the major preoccupation now for donors should be that of exploring ways to marshal the international political will to scale up aid flows...there is clear evidence that a substantial scaling up to all countries is possible, provided the necessary political will can be harnessed.'
Dr Ngozi Okonjo-Iweala, Minister of Finance, Nigeria, October 2004

Funding the Millennium Development Goals – by cancelling the debt of the poorest nations and allocating 0.7 per cent of national incomes to aid for poor countries – would incur relatively little financial cost to donors. But rich countries continue to deliver little more than empty promises. If the donors were judged, like the recipient countries, by their record on fulfilling their commitments, then their credit ratings would have gone through the floor.

In relative terms, donor countries devote a pittance of their wealth to aid budgets – which include the costs of debt relief. Current aid levels are far lower than those that have been repeatedly promised, and lower as a proportion of national income than ever before. Yet financing the MDG targets would cost less each year than the money that rich-country governments routinely spend on defence. The cost to the donors may be relatively low, but the human price paid in the world's poorest nations is high.

The human cost of under-funding

People in poverty pay a heavy price for rich countries' failure to provide the necessary finance for the MDGs. By 2015, if current trends continue[35] and targets are not met,

- 247 million more people in sub-Saharan Africa will be living on less than $1 a day
- 34 million more people in the world will go hungry
- 45 million more children will have died[36]
- 97 million more children will not be in school
- 98 million more people in sub-Saharan Africa will not have safe drinking water
- 53 million more people in the world will lack proper sanitation facilities.

The heaviest price will be paid by the people who are most vulnerable to poverty: women and children, members of ethnic minority groups, and people living with HIV/AIDS or disabilities.

Such appalling consequences reflect the fact that national and global plans are failing through lack of finance.

The poorest countries face financing shortages

Global estimates of the finance needed for developing countries to reach the MDGs range between $50 and $100 billion each year, in addition to existing aid budgets.[37] Countries such as Cambodia, Tanzania, and Ghana are among the poorest, ranking in the lowest third of countries according to the Human Development Index, which assesses life expectancy, education, and income per capita. Initial assessments suggest that to achieve the MDGs, Cambodia requires double its current levels of aid, Tanzania two-thirds more aid, and Ghana one-third more aid.[38]

Debt servicing still undermines public services

Despite eight years of the Highly Indebted Poor Countries (HIPC) initiative, only 40 per cent of those countries' combined debt has so far been cancelled.

Some of the poorest countries in the world still pay out more to their creditors than they spend on essential public services. Despite eight years of the Highly Indebted Poor Countries (HIPC) initiative – set up to deal comprehensively with the debt burden of 42 highly indebted nations – only 40 per cent of those countries' combined debt has so far been cancelled.[39] Interest payments have fallen on average, but in 2003 14 out of 27 countries receiving some form of debt relief under the initiative were still paying out more than 15 per cent of their total government revenue in interest.[40] The result: ten out of 14 African HIPC countries for which data are available are spending more on debt servicing than on health services. And countries such as Zambia – struggling to cope with the HIV/AIDS epidemic – spend more on debt servicing than on providing education: $150 million more in 2004 in Zambia's case.[41]

Water and sanitation sectors are deprived of resources

Around 50 per cent of rural dwellers in the least developed countries still have no access to improved water or sanitation facilities.[42] Yet annual aid allocated to improving water supplies and sanitation has fallen by more than $1 billion since the mid-1990s and is currently only half the estimated amount needed to meet the MDG goals.[43] In Madagascar and Mozambique, water supply is a priority sector for poverty-reduction efforts, but Mozambique requires around $18 million more each year to increase access to safe water, while Madagascar faces a funding gap of nearly $100 million each year if it is to meet the MDG water and sanitation targets.[44]

International education initiative is starved of cash

Around the world, approximately 104 million children who should be in school are not getting an education. The majority of them are girls. The Fast Track Initiative was set up by donors in 2002 with the explicit aim of ensuring international finance for all developing countries that produced good education plans. So far the initiative is failing – principally because the necessary cash is not being made available. Burkina Faso, Honduras, Mozambique, Niger, and Yemen have all had their plans endorsed by Fast Track, but find themselves short of the funds needed for 2004 and 2005.[45] More broadly, aid to primary education is a fraction of what is needed to ensure primary education for all – with only $1.4 billion being provided, compared with the $7 billion required each year.

Global health fund is under-resourced

In 2001 the Global Fund to Fight AIDS, TB, and Malaria was founded as a public–private partnership to raise new resources for prevention, care, and treatment programmes in countries where the needs are greatest. The fund has so far made grants to 127 countries to put 1.6 million people on anti-retroviral treatment for HIV, provide counselling and testing services, and support AIDS orphans. But the scale of the problem is far greater: six million people in the world today need treatment, and infection rates are still rising in sub-Saharan Africa. Despite this urgency, the Fund lacks resources. Money pledged so far for 2005 is only one quarter of the amount needed. And, although global spending on the fight against HIV/AIDS has risen, it is still less than half of what will be needed by developing countries by 2007.[46]

Small change: the current cost of aid

The problem is not that the financial demands of poverty reduction are overwhelming – but that the amount spent in the richest nations on tackling global poverty is shamefully small. By 2003, spending on aid and debt relief to all developing countries, measured per person in rich countries, was just $80 per year. For rich countries, this is small change: equivalent to just $1.53 from each person per week – or the price of a cup of coffee.

This small change is coming out of big pockets: the world's richest countries have never enjoyed so much wealth, with so little willingness to share it. The increase in rich-country incomes over the past forty years was unmatched by equivalent increases in aid.
While personal incomes in rich countries have grown by 200 per cent since 1960, official aid given per person has risen by only 50 per cent.

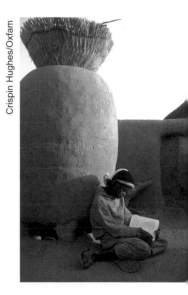

Crispin Hughes/Oxfam

Zenabu Zeba (aged 11) revising lessons at home in Nida village, Burkina Faso

Figure 3: Rich countries – more wealthy, less generous

Gross national income (GNI) and net official development assistance (ODA) per capita 1960-2003 at 2002 prices, OECD countries, 100=1960 value

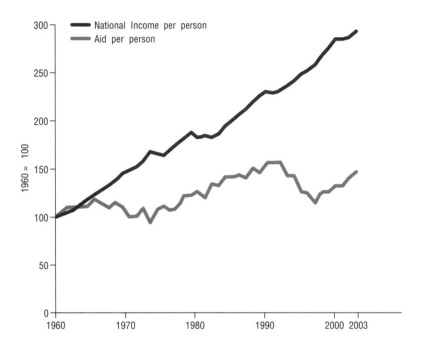

(Source: compiled by Oxfam from DAC data)

The result is that aid as a proportion of national income has collapsed. In the years 1960–65, rich countries spent 0.48 per cent of their combined national incomes on official development assistance. By 1980–85 they were spending just 0.34 per cent. By 2003, the proportion had dropped to 0.24 per cent (see Figure 4).

Figure 4: Governments spend less than ever on aid

Net ODA as percentage of GNI 1960-2003, OECD countries

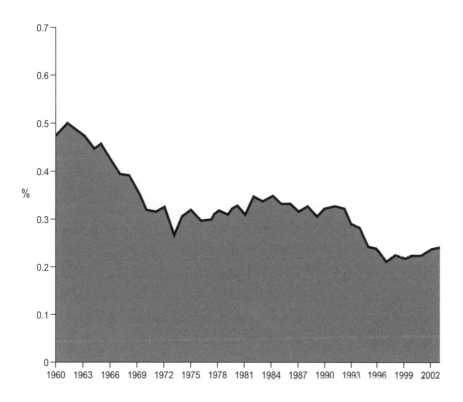

(Source: compiled by Oxfam from DAC data)

The decline in aid levels witnessed during the 1990s is now levelling off, and absolute aid levels have risen each year since 1997. But aid as a share of national income still remains below the levels of the early 1990s.[47]

The decline in aid flows is even more starkly evident in relation to the internationally recognised UN target of allocating 0.7 per cent of national income to development assistance – a target agreed in 1970. Of the 22 major bilateral donors, just five countries – Norway, Denmark, Netherlands, Luxembourg, and Sweden – currently meet the 0.7 per cent target.[48] None of the G7 donors – who account for nearly three-quarters of all aid – has ever met it (see Figure 5).

Figure 5: Most donors fall short of the UN's 0.7 per cent target

Net ODA as percentage of GNI and in absolute terms, by OECD donor, 2003 preliminary data

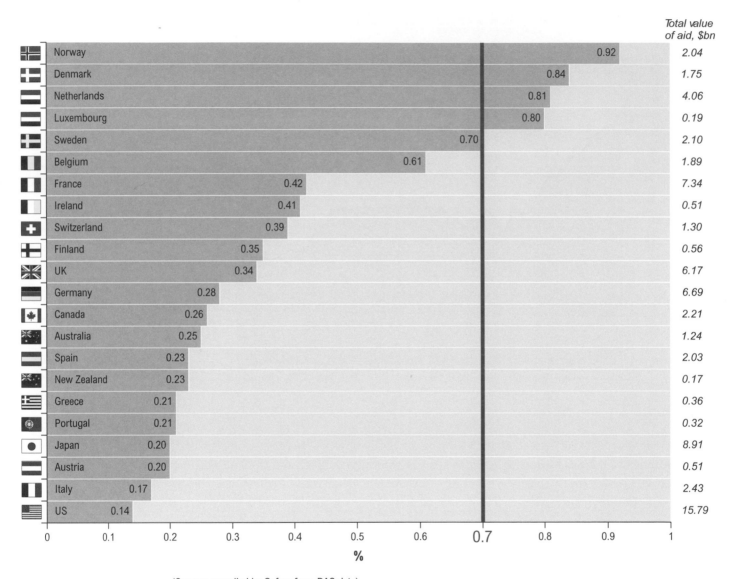

(Source: compiled by Oxfam from DAC data)

Although 12 out of the 22 OECD donors increased their absolute aid levels in 2003, for many of the biggest donors meeting the UN target of 0.7 per cent is not even on their agenda yet. Spain and the UK have recently drawn up timetables, but, as Table 2 shows, more than half of the OECD donors have no timetable for reaching the target. The recent decision by Ireland to abandon its plans to meet the target by 2007 highlights the fragility of such commitments.

Table 2: Off track…and without a plan

Donors already meeting 0.7 per cent target	Donors with a timetable for meeting 0.7 per cent target		Donors with no timetable
Norway	Belgium	(2010)	US
Denmark	Finland	(2010)	Italy
Netherlands	France	(2012)	Austria
Luxembourg	Spain	(2012)	Japan
Sweden	UK	(2013)	Portugal
			Greece
			New Zealand
			Australia
			Canada
			Germany
			Switzerland
			Ireland

The largest G7 donors appear to be in no hurry to meet the MDG goals set for 2015. If the trends experienced between 2001 and 2003 continue, they will not reach the 0.7 per cent target until the deadline has long gone.

- Canada will not reach 0.7 until 2025.

- It will be 2040 before the USA reaches 0.7.

- Germany will not reach 0.7 until 2087.

- It will take Italy until 2111 to reach 0.7.

- Japan seems unlikely ever to reach the target, given that it is reducing its aid budget.[49]

Recent donors' pledges to increase their aid fail to fill the gap. It is clear that the money promised will not be sufficient to meet minimal MDG costings, let alone the 0.7 per cent target. At the Monterrey Financing for Development Conference in 2002, the USA and EU did pledge aid increases which would take the global aid budget to around $75 billion in 2006. But this is at least $25 billion short of the minimum needed each year to reach the MDGs. And it still amounts to a collective total of only 0.29 per cent of national incomes, far below the target of 0.7 per cent.[50]

Pledges made beyond 2006 are no more encouraging. Those from EU governments would only take the global aid budget to 0.44 per cent of national income by 2010,[51] while the EU currently faces the challenge of raising its collective total beyond 2006.

And then pledges must be acted upon. The USA has so far failed to obtain congressional approval for all its Monterrey pledges,[52] and in the EU, despite commitments made on paper, three of the member states have made significant reductions in their aid expenditure.

Not only is aid under-funded, but it is being diverted by donors. Rich countries which promised debt relief for the poorest indebted countries are currently funding it out of their existing aid budgets, thereby reducing resources for other priorities and other countries. This approach to 'dropping the debt' is deceptive: the most indebted countries gain, but the poorest countries as a whole do not. The practice is deeply unfair: the money is found by diverting aid intended for less indebted but equally poor countries to those that are more deeply indebted. And it ignores a key premise of debt cancellation: that creditor governments should pay, in recognition of their part in creating the debt crisis. Instead, other low-income countries, not creditors themselves, are paying the price of creditors' past actions.

Kenya: setting off across a sewage-laden stream to buy water in the shanty community of Kibera, Nairobi.

Crispin Hughes/Oxfam

A history of broken promises

All of this amounts to a long history of broken promises. Rich nations have time and again signed international statements pledging to increase aid budgets to 0.7 per cent of their national income and end the problem of unsustainable debt. Time and again, they have failed to deliver on their own commitments.

Figure 6: Pledges to increase aid and debt relief: the rhetoric and the reality

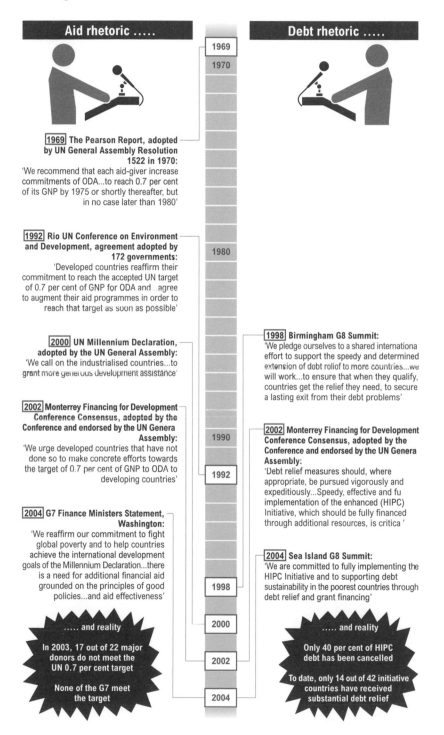

Aid rhetoric .....

1969 The Pearson Report, adopted by UN General Assembly Resolution 1522 in 1970:
'We recommend that each aid-giver increase commitments of ODA...to reach 0.7 per cent of its GNP by 1975 or shortly thereafter, but in no case later than 1980'

1992 Rio UN Conference on Environment and Development, agreement adopted by 172 governments:
'Developed countries reaffirm their commitment to reach the accepted UN target of 0.7 per cent of GNP for ODA and...agree to augment their aid programmes in order to reach that target as soon as possible'

2000 UN Millennium Declaration, adopted by the UN General Assembly:
'We call on the industrialised countries...to grant more generous development assistance'

2002 Monterrey Financing for Development Conference Consensus, adopted by the Conference and endorsed by the UN Genera Assembly:
'We urge developed countries that have not done so to make concrete efforts towards the target of 0.7 per cent of GNP to ODA to developing countries'

2004 G7 Finance Ministers Statement, Washington:
'We reaffirm our commitment to fight global poverty and to help countries achieve the international development goals of the Millennium Declaration...there is a need for additional financial aid grounded on the principles of good policies...and aid effectiveness'

..... and reality

In 2003, 17 out of 22 major donors do not meet the UN 0.7 per cent target

None of the G7 meet the target

Debt rhetoric .....

1998 Birmingham G8 Summit:
'We pledge ourselves to a shared internationa effort to support the speedy and determined extension of debt relief to more countries...we will work...to ensure that when they qualify, countries get the relief they need, to secure a lasting exit from their debt problems'

2002 Monterrey Financing for Development Conference Consensus, adopted by the Conference and endorsed by the UN Genera Assembly:
'Debt relief measures should, where appropriate, be pursued vigorously and expeditiously...Speedy, effective and fu implementation of the enhanced (HIPC) Initiative, which should be fully financed through additional resources, is critica '

2004 Sea Island G8 Summit:
'We are committed to fully implementing the HIPC Initiative and to supporting debt sustainability in the poorest countries through debt relief and grant financing'

..... and reality

Only 40 per cent of HIPC debt has been cancelled

To date, only 14 out of 42 initiative countries have received substantial debt relief

1969 1970 1980 1990 1992 1998 2000 2002 2004

Affordable for the affluent

Rich countries can well afford what it takes to achieve the MDGs, by cancelling the debt burden of the poorest countries that need it if they are to reach the MDGs, by meeting the 0.7 target, and by backing other suggested options to generate new aid money as soon as possible.

Cancelling the debt burden

Low-income countries are still paying out $100 million every day to their creditors.

Current debt-relief initiatives are not working well enough to deliver the fresh start that the poorest countries need. Low-income countries are still paying out $100 million every day to their creditors. And not only do interest payments continue to divert revenue away from the delivery of basic social services in HIPC countries, but, even when eligible countries have passed through the HIPC process, many still find themselves with debt levels classified as 'unsustainable' by the initiative itself.[53] And there is still no formal mechanism to tackle the debt burden in the developing countries that fall outside the HIPC initiative.[54]

Instead, debt should be cancelled for those low-income countries that are clearly unable to repay, and for whom debt repayments are limiting their ability to finance the MDGs. Indeed, any notion of what constitutes 'sustainable' debt levels should be based on what countries need in order to finance the MDGs, with attention paid to providing future aid in the form of grants, not loans, where necessary and monitoring the use of export credits to avoid creating new debt burdens. Given the efficacy of debt relief as a form of finance – it is stable, predictable, and delivered straight to government budgets – such a cancellation should be adopted as the first step in support for indebted low-income countries,[55] followed by increased aid.

Many of the OECD donors have already agreed to cancel their share of the bilateral (government-to-government) debt owed to them by the HIPC countries and some other low-income countries.[56] But only 50 per cent or less of multilateral debt has been cancelled to date, and it now constitutes most of the outstanding debt. In fact, as bilateral donors have been increasing resources dedicated to debt cancellation, the World Bank and IMF have simply reduced their contributions by an equivalent amount.

Without increased commitments from their shareholders, further action by the World Bank and other regional development banks to cancel debts – of which the largest is owed to the African Development Bank – would have to come from profits earned on lending to middle-income countries. Not only is it unfair to expect Brazil or Mexico to pay for the debt relief of the poorest countries, it does not make sense, given the millions of poor people also living in these so-called middle-income countries. Instead, rich-country shareholders must provide the extra resources to fund further debt cancellation – a step recently taken by the UK government, which agreed to finance multilateral debt service to the World Bank and African Development Bank until 2015 for 32 of the world's poorest countries.

Figures compiled by Oxfam show what other rich-country donors would have to pay if they followed the UK example.[57] Just $1.8 billion more would be needed every year from now until 2015: $2.10 per person per year in an OECD country. The cost to the UK, which has already pledged to do this, is higher than that to any other G7 nation – although the UK commitment is not currently additional to existing aid resources (see Figure 7).

Unlike the World Bank and regional development banks, however, the IMF does have the resources to finance such a cancellation. It controls the third-largest gold reserve in the world, which is currently undervalued to the tune of more than $30 billion (see Box 3).

Figure 7: The personal price of debt cancellation in G7 countries

Cost per person in G7 countries per year to 2015 of cancelling World Bank and African Development Bank debt for 32 of the world's poorest countries, US$

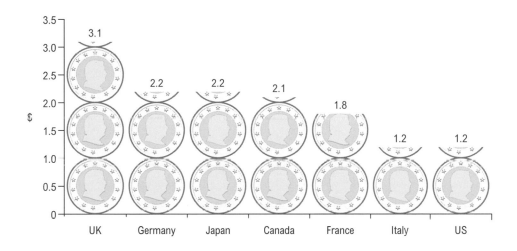

(Sources: Oxfam, compiled from World Bank data and based on UK Treasury figure of £100 million in cost per annum to the UK)

Box 3: A golden opportunity – using IMF gold to cancel debt

The IMF holds the third-largest reserve of gold in the world, which is linked to price levels prevalent when the IMF first acquired the gold. Since then, market prices for gold have risen dramatically, and, given the collapse of the Gold Standard in the early 1970s, the IMF neither needs nor uses its reserves. A revaluation or sale of the reserves would make money for the IMF – money that could be used for debt cancellation. It is estimated that such a transaction could raise more than $30 billion – more than it would cost both the World Bank and IMF to cancel the remaining debts of all HIPC countries.*

The IMF has revalued some gold stocks before, in 1999/2000, to finance the first round of relief under the HIPC initiative. A complex 'off-market' transaction was undertaken to minimise the effect on world gold prices – important to the profits of gold producers in developing and developed countries. A further sale or revaluation would have to be managed in a similar way. The impact of an open sale on world gold prices and thus on the livelihoods of miners in the developing world could be reduced if it were phased over a number of years and undertaken transparently. **

* The gold is valued at $8.5 billion at historical prices, but the market value is nearer $42 billion. See Kapoor 2004 for details.

** A recent study shows that the world gold price has been increasing, despite sales of large amounts of gold by central banks. It also shows that in the 1990s uncertainty about gold sales, not the actual sale itself, had the greatest impact on gold prices (Kapoor 2004).

The World Bank and IMF claim that to cancel multilateral debts would damage their status as respected creditors. But for the IMF the amount needed for a debt write-off represents a tiny proportion of its overall capital. And the unique status of both the Bank and the IMF among financial institutions – backed by explicit guarantees from donor governments – means that they are far more able in financial terms to bear the cost of drawing a line under the debts of poor countries.[58]

Delivering the 0.7 per cent target

Delivering now on commitments to meet the UN's target of devoting 0.7 per cent of national income to aid is still necessary, in addition to debt cancellation, to release ample resources to help the poorest countries to meet the MDG goals, with additional finance to pursue more ambitious poverty-reduction objectives.[59] If the 22 major donors had devoted 0.7 per cent of their combined national income to aid in 2003, the total global aid budget would have been $190 billion, instead of the actual figure of $70 billion.[60]

The difference of $120 billion would be enough to provide the additional $50–$100 billion needed each year to reach the MDG goals, and to fund other global priorities such as humanitarian assistance, international peacekeeping, and other challenges which require a global response: tackling health crises such as HIV/AIDS, and combating environmental degradation.

Delivering aid on this scale is by no means unprecedented: over four years, at the end of World War II, the USA invested at least $75 billion (in today's terms) in the Marshall Plan – about 2 per cent of its national income.[61] Nor would it be too expensive when compared with the current expenditures of rich countries and consumers:

- The additional $120 billion needed each year to reach 0.7 per cent is around one fifth of rich countries' spending on defence in 2003, and one half of rich countries' annual spending on subsidies to their own farmers. It is one quarter of the amount spent globally on advertising in 2002.

- Around $20–25 billion is needed each year to meet the MDGs in Africa – as much as the USA, the UK, and France together spend on arms exports to the developing world, and less than global consumers spend on cosmetics and perfume every year.

Figure 8: The price of poverty reduction in perspective

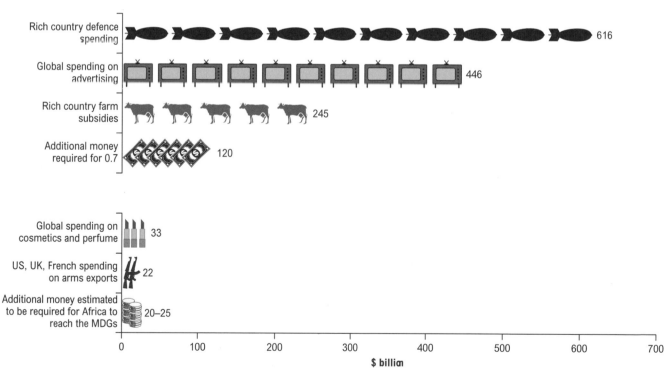

(Sources: International Institute for Strategic Studies, Oxfam International, Amnesty International, Development Assistance Committee of the OECD, African Development Bank, Worldwatch Institute)

The USA has the opportunity to make the biggest impact by reaching 0.7, given its currently low ratio of aid to income. Is it too much to ask of the world's richest country? The additional cost of meeting the 0.7 per cent target is small in relation to its other spending priorities:

- less than half of the cost so far of the war in Iraq

- one-sixth of the cost of general US defence expenditure.

Figure 9: US spending priorities

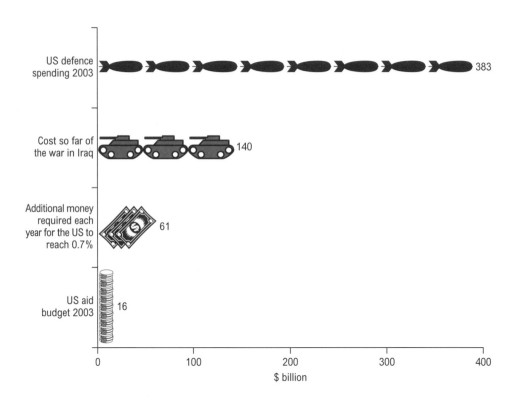

(Sources: International Institute for Strategic Studies, costofwar.com, OECD Development Assistance Committee)

Uganda: collapsing classroom walls at Kanyunyu Primary School

Backing alternative proposals for delivering aid

Besides action to reach the target of 0.7 per cent, proposals for other initiatives to release additional aid for poverty reduction are now on the table and should be taken forward by donor countries. Although donors should move to reach 0.7 per cent as soon as possible, additional resources need to be made available immediately, to deliver adequate volumes of aid in time for the MDGs to be reached. Many of these proposals for new financing mechanisms are also designed to guarantee better-quality, long-term, and predictable aid – which is often difficult to provide under current bilateral and multilateral arrangements.

The UK's proposal for an International Finance Facility (IFF) would use the money pledged by donors at the 2002 Monterrey Conference as collateral for issuing bonds on international markets. Pledges ostensibly made for the future would therefore release money that could be spent now – potentially up to $50 billion a year until 2015.[62] The IFF is a welcome means of raising urgently needed resources, but if its implementation is to gain wider support, detailed information is needed about the means of administering it, and methods of ensuring that the funds will be used effectively for poverty reduction. Furthermore, the initiative must be developed on the understanding that payments are additional to 0.7 per cent, so that development budgets in donor countries beyond 2015 – when the Facility ends – are not reduced in order to finance IFF repayments.

Other innovative suggestions, such as global taxation, have been proposed through the Global Fund Against Hunger and Poverty, launched by the French, Spanish, Brazilian, and Chilean governments in September 2004 and supported by more than 50 others.[63] They include the introduction of a small tax on financial transactions, a tax on carbon emissions, a tax on arms sales, and the use of international reserves held by IMF member countries. Many of these proposals, unlike the IFF, have no cut-off date and could complement the use of the IFF, if activated to function beyond 2015. Some, such as the use of international reserves, require universal participation for their implementation; but even those that do not, such as a financial transactions tax, still require a more widespread agreement to be effective – and more donors should endorse the principle as part of their plans for financing global poverty eradication.[64]

3
Value for money: how donors can make aid work better

Zambia: villagers in Siavonga District collecting water from Lake Kariba

3
Value for money: how donors can make aid work better

'While we are supposed to implement policy, we are producing papers.'
Ministry of Education official, Tanzania, June 2004

Aid works – but it could work much better. More finance is clearly needed, but it needs to be better delivered too, by donors and developing-country governments alike. Part 4 of this report will focus on the role of developing-country governments; Part 3 illustrates how donors often prevent aid working as well as it should for the benefit of people living in poverty.

In the most notorious cases, donors have used aid to support political regimes which have no interest in the welfare of their citizens. But to claim that increases in aid are not justified because of the existence of poor practice is akin to closing down all international companies on the basis of the Enron scandal. The argument ignores good aid practice, which illustrates that problems are not endemic to the aid system but are a result of its mismanagement, by rich-country donors and by developing-country recipients. In any case, poor aid practice in the past does not necessarily mean poor aid practice in the future. The fact that change is possible is evidenced by shifts in thinking about aid over the past decade: donors now prioritise poverty reduction to a greater extent and are more likely to support recipient governments' choices about the best use of aid money. Reform of the way in which aid is delivered can and must be accompanied by vital increases in aid budgets.

Rich-country donors are still failing to make aid work most effectively for poor people on at least three counts:

- Aid is allocated according to donors' strategic interests, not in response to the needs of poor people.

- Burdensome management requirements are imposed on recipient countries, while deliveries of aid are highly uncertain, undermining the recipient government's ability to plan and implement poverty-reduction programmes.

- Conditions are attached to aid programmes which leave little room for recipient countries to define their own reform paths; the appropriateness and sustainability of aid programmes are thereby compromised.

Donors have made commitments to change in all of these areas – but many are failing to live up to their promises. Such failure threatens public confidence in the effectiveness of the entire aid system, but, as the good practices of some donors show, failure is not inevitable.

Strategise – but for poverty reduction

When aid giving becomes politicised, poor people lose out. The history of overseas assistance includes some appalling political acts, perpetrated in the guise of aid. Yet still today, long after the Cold War era, the agendas of many donors are driven by their own domestic and foreign-policy concerns. Studies have demonstrated that an historic colonial link remains a major determinant of aid flows.[65]

As Table 3 demonstrates, the most favoured recipients of G7 aid in 2002 were not necessarily the poorest. Donors prefer to publicise the aid that they give in the form of Official Development Assistance (ODA), which goes to countries defined as 'traditional' developing nations; but they also make aid available on the same terms to Eastern European countries and other developing nations that are considered to be more 'advanced' in their development.[66] Taking the two categories of aid together reveals the truth about donors' real priorities. Two of the top recipients of French aid, French Polynesia and New Caledonia, and Israel, one of the top recipients of US aid, are classified as high-income countries. France's priorities appear to be determined by colonial ties, those of the USA by strategic considerations, and Japan's by regional interests.[67]

The problem is not confined to bilateral donors. Over the past decade, the European Commission has prioritised regional security above global poverty reduction, allocating greater shares of aid to neighbouring Mediterranean and Eastern European countries. In 2002, Poland, Romania, and Hungary were the top recipients of its total aid budget, while low-income countries received only 37 per cent of its ODA.[68]

In 2002, one-third of the increase in aid flows came from large allocations to Afghanistan and Pakistan.

The 'war on terror' threatens to revive an era when aid was diverted for strategic aims. Firstly, aid has again been used as a political tool, as proved by the exercise in persuading key voters on the UN Security Council to support the war on Iraq, when the USA, the UK, and France put pressure on wavering African nations with whom they have significant aid relationships.[69] Secondly, aid is again being allocated, and reallocated, on the basis of narrow 'security' concerns. In 2002, one-third of the increase in aid flows came from large allocations to Afghanistan and Pakistan.[70] The USA has levered around $32 billion in supplemental aid budgets over the past three years to fund Afghanistan and its neighbours as well as reconstruction in Iraq. Total US aid flows to strategically important countries (Israel, Egypt, Jordan, Iraq, and Turkey) and to Afghanistan and its neighbours over the past three years are roughly equal to US aid to the rest of the world combined.[71] In the UK, aid promised to poor and marginalised groups in middle-income countries has been diverted into funds for reconstruction in Afghanistan and Iraq, while in Canada vast aid commitments to Afghanistan

Table 3: G7 donors' favourite aid recipients: failing to prioritise the poorest

Average income per capita (PPP, 2003 estimates) of the top three recipients of gross aid (ODA and Official Aid (OA)) in absolute terms, 2002

Donor		Top 3 recipients of aid	Recipients' average annual income per capita
France	1st 2nd 3rd	Cote d'Ivoire French Polynesia New Caledonia	$11300
USA	1st 2nd 3rd	Egypt Russia Israel	$10833
Canada	1st 2nd 3rd	Poland Former Yugoslavia Cameroon	$6376
Japan	1st 2nd 3rd	China India Thailand	$5100
Germany	1st 2nd 3rd	Serbia and Montenegro China Bolivia	$3233
UK	1st 2nd 3rd	India Serbia & Montenegro Tanzania	$1933
Italy	1st 2nd 3rd	Mozambique Tanzania Eritrea	$833

Average income per capita in the world's poorest countries*	$1307

* Least developed countries

(Source: compiled by Oxfam from Development Assistance Committee 2004, Human Development Report 2004, CIA Factbook 2004)

and Iraq may have undermined commitments to Africa and other low-income 'priority' countries.[72] Finally, the very goals of development aid are being redefined to suit the new security agenda: in Denmark, Japan, and Australia, 'combating terrorism' has become an explicit aim of official aid programmes.

Investment in Afghani and Iraqi reconstruction is obviously essential – and still lacks effective finance. But a new era of political aid-giving, driven by such narrow concerns for the donors' own security, poses a real threat to efforts to reduce global poverty. It will divert aid away from the poorest countries and communities, and weaken donors' commitment to poverty reduction.

Domestic interests are also high on many donors' aid agendas. Nearly one-third of aid finance from the G7 is 'tied': conditional on the purchase of goods and services from the donor country. Applying this condition to aid knocks an estimated 20–30 per cent off the value of aid flows for developing countries.[73] As the experience of Nicaragua makes clear (see Box 4), tied aid prevents developing countries from putting their money to best use, and denies them the option of hiring domestic suppliers.

Box 4: Strings attached – Spanish aid to Nicaragua

Nicaragua is a major beneficiary of projects overseen by Spain's Overseas Development Fund (FAD), which finances hospital construction, transport, and roads. '*Nicaragua needs aid*,' says Alejandro Terán, President of the Chamber for Construction in Nicaragua, '*but not tied aid*'. Spanish contractors and machinery cost more than local competitors or those from third countries. The head of the Ministry of Health in San Juan de Dios, where hospital construction and equipment has been paid for by FAD, comments: '*The price of the equipment was overvalued. It could have been bought from other countries at half the price.*' Much of the equipment is said to have been sub-standard and to have lasted for less than six months in the hospital.

Tied aid deprives local companies of employment opportunities. Nelda Hernández, Director of Planning in the Ministry for Transport and Infrastructure, says, '*These kinds of loan create ill feeling in the country's businesses, who feel money should be going to them. Local businesses should be allowed to participate more.*' Nicaragua is clearly not benefiting from the full value of aid. To quote Terán again, '*Foreign companies could come and give us a little bit of the cake, but instead they come to subcontract us for pitiful sums and take all the profits home to Spain.*'

(Source: La Realidad de la Ayuda 2004/2005 , Intermón Oxfam)

In 2001, DAC donors agreed to untie their aid to Least Developed Countries 'to the greatest extent possible',[74] a commitment that was upheld in the Monterrey Declaration. Of the 22 major donor countries, six – Belgium, Finland, Ireland, Norway, Switzerland, and the UK – have now almost or completely done so. However, Italy, the USA, and Canada still seem determined to gain from what they give (see Figure 10). Further, the DAC agreement excludes Technical Co-operation – namely the provision of consultants and research services – and food aid, which are significant portions of total aid budgets.

Figure 10: Aid for whom? G7 donors still serve their own domestic interests

Percentage of aid (ODA) that is tied, excluding Technical Co-operation and administration costs, 2002 or latest available data

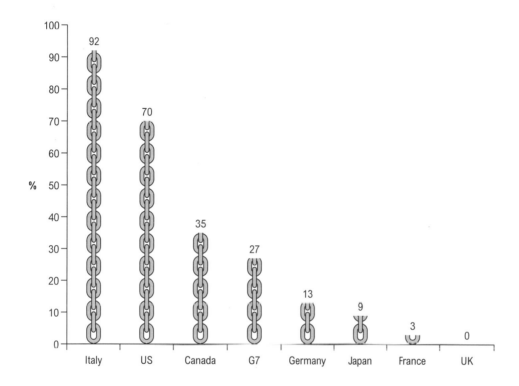

Note: this does not include 'partially tied' aid, contingent on purchase from either the donor country or another developing country.

(Source: compiled by Oxfam from DAC and OECD data, and based on Congressional Research Service estimates of US tying)

Technical Co-operation may be excluded from the data used in Figure 10, but it is too often tied to the employment of advisers from donor countries. The three main recipients of Australian contracts are Australian, while recent analysis by ActionAid reveals that the top ten recipients of British Technical Assistance contracts are UK and Canadian multinational companies.[75] And it forms a large proportion of donor budgets: it accounts for 40 per cent of the bilateral aid budget, and the proportion is rising.[76] While such consultancies can bring expertise to countries with shortages of skilled personnel, if their use is donor-driven in this way the value of aid money is reduced, and the recipient government's freedom to appoint advisers is restricted.

The lasting impact on local staff development and institutions remains largely unevaluated.[77] An Oxfam survey of donor practices (see below) found that many donors are still unwilling to use local consultants and, probably as a result, in 70 per cent of cases reported in the survey the amount of money spent on consultancy was described as 'too much' or 'excessive'.

Scrutiny of aid budgets reveals that far less actually reaches developing countries than might be expected. As Figure 11 shows, by the time donors have paid their consultants, covered their administration expenses, and included the costs of commitments such as debt relief and support for refugees in their own countries, the remaining transfer of aid to developing countries is a mere 40 per cent of the total budget.

Figure 11: Revealed: where the aid budget really goes
Breakdown of aid (net ODA) by purpose, 2002

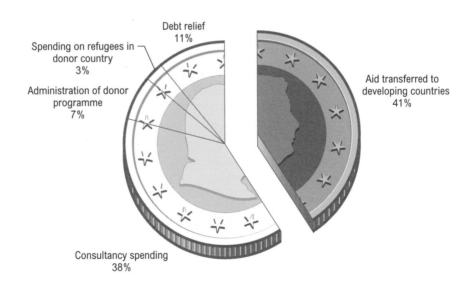

(Source: compiled by Oxfam from DAC data)

Cut the red tape

Managing donors and their projects is a time-consuming task. In Tanzania in 2002–03, the government received 275 donor missions, of which 123 were World Bank missions, conducted by a total of 516 World Bank staff. Twenty out of 39 donor agencies submitted no information about their project or programme spending when requested by the government to do so.

Too often donors are guilty of the following unhelpful practices:

- Insisting on their own, often complex, management procedures, failing to co-ordinate with the recipient governments or other donors, and delaying the release of finance when governments cannot comply.

- Failing to inform the host government about their activities in the country.

- Providing finance on a short-term basis only.

- Making commitments which do not reflect what is actually delivered.[78]

These problems can seem far removed from the central question of how to make aid work for poor communities. But making aid work for national governments is critical to this end. The poor practices listed above restrict the time available for government officials to design, manage, and implement national programmes; and they limit the opportunities for long-term, effective planning in countries where skilled personnel are few (see Box 5). Donors all too often fail to create a sense of partnership between themselves and recipient governments, and they reduce the sense of national ownership by preventing governments from making their own decisions about the expenditure of aid.

Box 5: The costs of managing aid in Ethiopia

Both government and donor officials in Ethiopia acknowledge numerous problems with aid-related procedures. Recent research by Oxfam found the following problems.

- Donors fail to inform recipient governments about their spending plans or report how much they have spent. One World Bank country review noted: 'The team were struck time and time again by the incompleteness of information available to the government on aid expenditures.'

- While the Ethiopian government's financial year begins in July, European donors begin their planning cycle in January, leaving half the year uncoordinated. During this time, it is virtually impossible for the government to draw on donors' funds. High turnover among the staff of donor departments can also block progress: *'We feel we've agreed policies, and then someone comes three weeks later and says it's awful'*, explained one government official. Donors' lengthy vetting of government procurement plans adds delay: the EU reportedly delayed one road-building project by five months in this way.

- The disbursement of funding from IDA, the soft-loan arm of the World Bank, to the education sector illustrates how cumbersome donor procedures can exacerbate the problems experienced by over-stretched national bureaucracies in managing aid money. The Ministry of Finance receives the funds and releases them to the Ministry of Education and regional authorities. In turn, they submit an array of monthly reports, including requests for budget transfers to the Treasury, financial reports for the Ministry, a separate set for IDA, and statements of expenditure. Until all these are received, the Ministry of Finance cannot apply to Washington for the next payment, which must be signed by the Minister and must include details of expenditure signed by all the relevant personnel. The whole process should take less than 90 days, to ensure that there are always sufficient funds for the next 90 days of activities. In practice, the procedure typically takes around seven months.

(Source: Fraser for Oxfam GB, 2004)

Donors have publicly declared their intention to change their ways. At the Monterrey Financing for Development Conference in 2002, they committed themselves to reduce the burden of aid management on developing-country governments and to support policy priorities driven by developing countries themselves.[79] Following that, a meeting in 2003 of major bilateral donor agencies – including G7 donor governments and multilateral institutions such as the World Bank – to discuss reform of aid practices resulted in the 'Rome Declaration', which recognised that issues of donor requirements and processes 'require urgent, coordinated and sustained action to improve our effectiveness on the ground'.[80] The signatories made the following commitments:

- To deliver aid in accordance with the priorities, systems, and procedures of the developing countries.

- To adopt common procedures for the planning, management, and delivery of aid (for example, through allocations to particular sectors).

- To reduce the numbers of missions, reviews, reports, and conditions.

- To be transparent about their activities.

- To foster staff recognition of these principles in the interests of aid effectiveness.

And yet, interviews with recipient-government officials, conducted by Oxfam in mid-2004, indicate that many donors have still not put these principles into practice. The survey of donor practice, carried out anonymously in 11 countries across Africa, Asia, the Middle East, and Eastern Europe,[81] found the following.

- In 52 per cent of reported cases, government officials spend 'too much' or 'excessive' amounts of time reporting to donors.

- In 50 per cent of reported cases, none or only some donor activities fitted with the government's financial planning.

- In 31 per cent of reported cases, donor aid arrives more than six months late.

- In 70 per cent of cases, donors commit aid for only three years or less, and in 10 per cent of those cases for less than six months. To guarantee a complete primary education for one generation of children, school funding would be needed for six years.

The costs of aid remain high, with government officials making observations such as the following:

- *'The complexity of procedure may extend the length of the programme by one or two years'* – government official in West Africa

- *'Due to the time dedicated to meetings and missions, central and regional directors are often absent from their posts, and this disrupts the flow of activities'* – government official in West Africa

- In Georgia it takes 43 full-time government staff to manage the process of reporting to donors.

As Table 4 demonstrates, across each area surveyed, the European Commission and the USA were consistently given the lowest ratings.

Table 4: The donor contest: how recipients rate donors' practice

	Simplifying reporting requirements	Delivering aid on time	Committing for the long-term	Fitting in with the government budget cycle	Imposing minimal conditions
Best score	UK	Japan	World Bank	Japan	Germany
2nd	EC	World Bank	Germany	World Bank	UK
3rd	Germany	UK	Japan	Germany	US
4th	Japan	Germany	UK	UK	EC
5th	World Bank	US	EC	EC	Japan
Worst	US	EC	US	US	World Bank

(Source: Oxfam survey of donor practice, 2004)

The difference in donors' performance was particularly obvious in terms of reporting requirements and the timely delivery of aid, as Figures 12 and 13 show. In 60 per cent of cases reported, respondents described the reporting requirements imposed by the World Bank and the USA as 'too much' or 'excessive', while in 69 per cent of cases the UK's reporting requirements were described as 'acceptable'. Of course, reporting on the use of aid is vital in order to ensure accountability – but donors should require this to be done at a minimum cost to the government systems that they aim to support.

In terms of delivering aid on time, the survey found that in 25 per cent of cases, aid disbursements arrived between six and twelve months late. However, as Figure 13 shows, ratings for the European Commission were far worse than the rest – with 20 per cent of its aid said to arrive more than one year late.

Figure 12: Bound in red tape – especially by the World Bank and the USA

Responses to the question 'How much of your ministry's time is spent in reporting to the donor?'

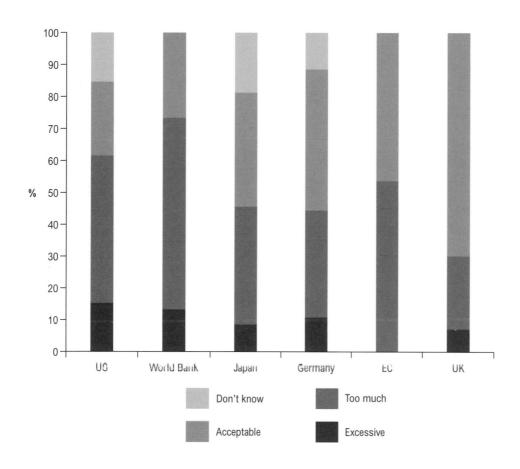

(Source: Oxfam survey of donor practice, 2004)

Figure 13: Expect delays in aid delivery – especially from the EC

Responses to the question 'Generally speaking, how late do the donor's aid disbursements arrive?'

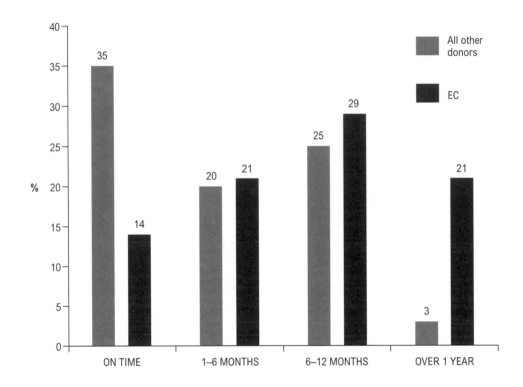

(Source: Oxfam survey of donor practice, 2004)

Respondents did, however, note some evidence of improvements, thanks to support for sectoral programmes and the introduction of budget support, or the routing of aid money directly through the government treasury. Increasingly, some donors are using these approaches, with donors such as Canada and Japan altering their legislation to facilitate it. And such approaches do make a difference: in Tanzania, the introduction of a sector plan and a pooled fund for primary education, in which nine donors work together to allocate funds, has radically altered ways of working. Before this, the Ministry of Education was fragmented into enclaves which negotiated separately with the different donors; for example, an English Language Unit was run in conjunction with the British Council, and a textbook unit was co-ordinated with the Swedish Development Agency. The Ministry knew very little about the nature of donors' projects in the sector. Now, in the words of one ministry official, '*There is more focused participation, and money is channelled in a manner that is more open*'. The enclaves have gone, and all activities are co-ordinated within one common framework.

More aid is also being provided to support national poverty-reduction strategy papers (PRSPs) produced by low-income countries – uniting donors behind one set of objectives – and other initiatives, such as the 'Three Ones', a set of principles launched by UNAIDS and endorsed by key donors, through which donors support a single national HIV/AIDS co-ordinating body, a single national strategy, and a single framework for monitoring and evaluation.[82]

However, the barriers to improving co-ordination – both with other donors and with governments – are high, given donors' desire to keep their own aid programmes visible and accountable to their domestic publics. Often, even where sectoral and budget-support structures are in place, elements of the previous style of behaviour persist. Ministry of Education officials in Tanzania identified a heavy burden of continuous reporting and a large amount of aid funding that never passes through the government budget. And although an international process is being led by the Development Assistance Committee to monitor improvements in donor practice, most of its recommendations are not binding on donors. Donors are quick to hold recipient governments to account for use of their funds, but there is very little to hold donors to account for their behaviour towards aid recipients. While initiatives such as independent monitoring groups and recipient-government reviews of donor practice do occur, they do so largely on an *ad hoc* and voluntary basis.

Support nationally defined poverty programmes

If aid is to be used effectively for poverty reduction, national policies need to be planned, formulated, and discussed by government, parliament, and civil society. Not only is such policy ownership a sovereign right, but it ensures that reform is tailored to local circumstances, enhancing its effectiveness and sustainability. This ownership is weakened when donors require large numbers of policy changes as a condition of aid money, and when they dominate analysis of the effects of recommended policy changes – trends that are exacerbated if donors co-ordinate their objectives and administration without commensurate changes to the way in which they interact with recipient governments.

In the 1980s and 1990s, increased numbers of conditions were imposed by donors, in an attempt to buy reform in developing countries. By the late 1990s, however, given concerns about the effectiveness of attaching so many conditions, donors tried to reduce their number and scope, to enable countries to choose their own policy-reform paths. The rhetoric of 'national ownership' has pervaded donor discourse. However, in practice, donors' imposition of economic conditions, coupled with other forms of policy influence, continues to weaken national ownership and increase the management burden of aid by attaching large numbers of conditions to funding programmes, prescribing specific reform paths; and by failing to base conditions on recipient countries' own plans and independent analysis, or support genuine choices between policy options.

The role of the IMF and World Bank is crucial in this regard. The IMF in particular plays 'gatekeeper' to other donors, who follow its advice about developing countries' macro-economic policies, with the result that developing countries must accept the IMF's conditions if they are to receive aid monies. And increasingly, bilateral donors giving budgetary support align their conditions with those designed by the IMF and World Bank.

Oxfam's analysis of the World Bank conditions tied to Poverty Reduction Support Credits (PRSCs) – the loans that support national poverty-reduction plans – found that, in three countries, governments are still required to carry out a high number of policy changes over one-year or two-year periods:

- In 2004–05, the Ethiopian government must complete 85 policy actions.

- In 2005–07, the Vietnamese government must complete 84.

- In 2004–05, the Tanzanian government must complete 78 policy changes for all its donors, with bilateral donors continually adding their own conditions to the original set attached to the World Bank PRSC.

In 60 per cent of cases recorded in the Oxfam survey of donors' practices, respondents described the number of World Bank conditions as 'large' or 'excessive'.

In 60 per cent of cases recorded in the Oxfam survey of donors' practices, respondents described the number of World Bank conditions as 'large' or 'excessive'; the Bank received the worst score of all the donors that were rated.

The IMF's process of reducing conditions, or 'streamlining', has been limited because the exercise applies only to one set of its conditions – so-called 'structural' conditions attached to institutional reforms such as privatisation – and not to 'macro-economic' conditions, which set targets for variables such as growth and inflation.[83] And only some countries have benefited; those judged to be poor performers have been largely excluded, despite being least able to manage large numbers of onerous conditions.[84]

A further problem is that many of the 'structural' conditions discontinued by the IMF have been adopted by the World Bank, or even by bilateral donors. And the IMF and World Bank now operate a policy of 'cross-conditionality', whereby IMF funds are dependent on progress towards meeting the Bank's conditions, and vice versa. Countries therefore find themselves more, not less, tightly constrained by the actions of both institutions.

Of course, the numbers of conditions do not tell the whole story: it is the content of such conditions that also limits the freedom of action of recipient governments. Certain policy options are still not acceptable to donors: the IMF itself states that to be successful, economic policy programmes should take account of a country's preference – but the choice may be made only from the 'viable policy options' presented by the political leadership and civil society; viability is presumably judged by the IMF.[85]

Although many of the structural adjustment reforms – liberalising trade, agriculture, and financial markets, privatising social services, and down-sizing government – have been completed, similar types of reform continue to be enshrined in loan agreements, without appropriate assessment of their impact on poverty reduction, or indeed the appropriate appraisal of the impact of past reforms. The privatisation of utilities remains a 'prominent condition' attached to the IMF and World Bank's individual project loans and economic-policy lending.[86] The IMF's continued over-emphasis on stabilisation also leads it to set tight public-spending targets – limits on government expenditure which restrict the degree of aid that a country can spend on public services. A recent Oxfam/EURODAD survey of IMF programmes in 20 countries found that countries such as Cameroon were set targets to achieve fiscal surplus, thereby restraining public expenditure, at the same time as plans to reduce infant mortality remained under-financed.[87] By the IMF's own admission, this policy is outdated, because in many countries stabilisation has been achieved, and fiscal restraint is less necessary.

Key documents are not publicly available, and discussion takes place behind closed doors.

The result is that participatory planning through Poverty Reduction Strategy Papers (PRSPs), introduced by the IMF and World Bank, is weakened, as decisions about national policy are taken elsewhere. While the PRSP process does represent the most concerted effort to date to persuade donors to support nationally owned plans for poverty reduction, donors have directly undermined it by continuing to negotiate conditionalities outside this framework. Instead of the IMF using the PRSP as the basis for its conditionalities, of the 20 countries with PRSPs completed by March 2003, 16 had IMF programmes agreed prior to the completion of the PRSP.[88] The potential for public debate is also limited when key documents recording agreements between governments and donors are not publicly available, and discussion takes place behind closed doors between donor officials and a small number of government officials – often without the involvement even of democratically elected parliaments. Despite commitments to better public disclosure, the World Bank still does not publish its Letters of Development Policy on a routine basis – documents which set out the government policies that it is proposing to support with Bank credits. Drafts of PRSCs and IMF Poverty Reduction and Growth Facility (PRGF) agreements should be publicly released, as should core documents related to all forms of programmatic lending, including all economic and sector work.

Crispin Hughes/Oxfam

Angola: the daily task of fetching water from a local spring in Malanje Province

Very little attempt is made to base conditions on independent analysis of the impact that various policy options are likely to have on poor people. Recent analysis of World Bank and IMF conditions to privatise the water system in Dar es Salaam, Tanzania, shows that, although women have primary responsibility for providing water, there was no consideration of gender in the design of the reform, and no effort was made to target women for consultation.[89]

Following considerable pressure from civil-society groups, the World Bank and IMF introduced an initiative intended to analyse their proposals' potential impact on poor communities. It is known as Poverty and Social Impact Analysis (PSIA). PSIA was to be done before a reform was chosen; it was supposed to be independent and to involve policy-formulation discussions with civil society and parliament. Unfortunately, three years later, and with 90 studies completed, PSIA is being conducted largely in secret, with a focus on the sequencing of reforms already agreed. In Malawi, the results of a PSIA on the privatisation of the state marketing board were withheld for two years, despite national debate about the board's role in food provision at the time of a food crisis. The analysis, which advised against privatisation before regulations to protect the poor were in place, was ignored in the conditions attached to a new loan by the World Bank. In Chad, the PSIA does nothing more than examine the different ways to privatise cotton marketing, rather than assessing the appropriateness of privatisation *per se*.[90]

PSIA has rapidly become one of innumerable studies produced by the IMF and World Bank – studies used to influence governments' policy choices. Since the introduction of the PRSP process, supposed to enhance government ownership of poverty-reduction plans, the production of World Bank 'knowledge' – studies produced at the country level – has actually increased.[91] For national authorities it is difficult to generate detailed counter-proposals to challenge what is often described as 'policy-based evidence', rather than 'evidence-based policy'.

While donors are entitled to account clearly for their aid money and to see that it is spent on broadly agreed poverty-reduction and gender-equity outcomes, this practice of imposing large numbers of detailed conditions and dominating analysis about the impact of policy reform discredits their rhetoric about the need for national ownership, and undermines the progress represented by the PRSP process in many countries.

4

Delivering development: how Southern governments can make aid work better

A community health worker checks a patient's blood pressure at a clinic in Burkina Faso

4
Delivering development: how Southern governments can make aid work better

'I can confidently say that the number of patients in these units has tripled ever since cost sharing [fees for health care] *was scrapped. The current policy of free health services should not be tampered with, since it mainly benefits the poor, who cannot afford expensive drugs in health clinics.'*
Chief for Masese, Jinja, Uganda[92]

In 2000, the Ugandan government abolished user fees for primary health care, giving poor people free access to clinics. The result: health units reported an increase of between 50 and 100 per cent in attendance almost overnight. Immunisation rates more than doubled. More than 50 per cent of the benefits went to the poorest fifth of the population. And the policy has catalysed further reforms, including a doubling of the health budget, faster budget releases, and higher pay for health workers.[93]

This policy is succeeding because it has clear government commitment, the backing of long term donor finance, and the participation of Uganda's vibrant civil society. The Ugandan Participatory Poverty Assessment (a joint study by government and civil society, showing the damage done by clinic charges to poor people's health) had turned user fees into an election issue in 2000 – and the government then fulfilled its election pledge. Now civil-society organisations track government spending, with monitoring committees established by the Uganda Debt Network in 12 districts to report on government spending and draw attention to cases of corruption.

Governments of developing countries, as well as donors, play a central role in delivering development and guaranteeing people's basic rights. It is their responsibility to provide basic services and ensure decent livelihoods for people living in poverty; to manage aid and public money equitably and effectively; and to be responsive and accountable to their citizens. As experience in Uganda shows, aid works best when it is channelled through national budgets focused on clear poverty-reduction goals and formulated with the involvement of civil society. Delivering services to poor people cannot be left solely to the private sector or NGOs. Only the public sector has the means and incentive to do this equitably and sustainably, and on a national basis.

Governments in developing countries are often universally characterised as ineffective and corrupt, lacking the capacity and commitment to use aid well. Undoubtedly, many governments have a long way to go to honour their responsibilities to their citizens: even Uganda, at the same time as having an excellent record on poverty reduction, has failed to protect civilians from violence by ending insecurity and conflict in the north of the country. Nevertheless, there has been substantial progress in the performance and accountability of many governments across the developing world.

To make this happen, and to ensure the most effective use of aid, governments of developing countries need to take vigorous action in two major respects:

- combat corruption and build effective institutions;

- deliver budgets and policies to benefit poor people.

Donors too must play their part – which includes supporting Southern government institutions as much as possible. Both governments and donors should act to foster a strong and critical civil society and national parliaments which perform effective checks on corruption and the nature of public spending.

Combat corruption and build effective institutions

Corruption exists in every country and undermines social justice in many. It diverts public money to rich elites; raids resources for poverty reduction; and distorts the economy — with the biggest impact felt by the poorest people.

Ghana:
Mark Hemans-Mensah
at work at Groove FM radio
station, Accra

Penny Tweedie/Oxfam

The good news is that the political conditions for tackling corruption and building accountable governments are improving across the developing world. Many countries are setting up democratic governments which are increasingly responsive to citizens. Elections, although an imperfect indicator of democracy, are nevertheless now more common across the developing world, since the peaceful end to authoritarian regimes in countries such as Indonesia, Bolivia, Nigeria, Madagascar, and Kenya.[94] In sub-Saharan Africa, multi-party elections have been held over the past decade in 44 out of 50 countries. A recent study in 28 African countries points also to high average voter turnouts and greater inclusiveness and diversity in political appointments.[95] Lastly, but crucially, a lively civil society and independent media are emerging in many of the poorest countries, demanding accountability from their governments. As the ownership of radio and TV has been liberalised in African countries, independent stations have sprung up in many places. In Ghana, call-in radio programmes and political commentary on 40 FM stations during the 2000 election increased voter turnout and reduced interference with polling.[96]

People in these new democracies are calling for an end to corruption and electing those who promise to tackle the problem. The anti-corruption campaign of Kenya's new government has brought a 25 per cent reduction in bribery since 2002[97] — although there is still much work to be done to repair the damage of decades. In Georgia, three weeks of non-violent protests by civil society against fraudulent parliamentary elections brought the resignation of Edward Shevardnadze from the presidency in November 2003. The new leader, Mikhail Saakashvili, has a strong popular mandate to fight corruption and economic stagnation. This enabled his government, after a mere six months in power, to improve tax revenue, raise the pay of customs officers, pay due pensions, and arrest corrupt officials in the public and private sectors.[98]

There are distinct types of corruption. 'Grand state corruption' – where elites capture public resources at the expense of most citizens – is not confined to developing countries. But in under-resourced, fledgling democracies with low levels of citizen awareness, the problems of grand state corruption are particularly serious. On the other hand, 'administrative corruption' – including minor bribery, nepotism, and low-level tax evasion – may be small-scale, but it is widespread and it adds up to substantial misallocation of resources. Poor people bear the brunt of petty forms of corruption, having to pay a greater share of their income in bribes than rich people do.[99] It both causes and results in inefficiency, and is due in part to the lack of investment in public institutions.

The following factors allow these forms of corruption to thrive:

- weak, co-opted, or unaccountable public institutions such as the judiciary, national audit offices, the media, and parliaments;

- under-resourced public sectors, staffed by inadequate numbers of poorly trained and under-paid civil servants;

- poor performance incentives: low salaries, weak management, and inadequate auditing within the civil service;

- low accountability of government to citizens and citizens' organisations.

In the worst cases, these factors can create a vicious circle whereby a culture of impunity leads to weak public sectors being co-opted by elites and paralysed by bribery, and an uninformed population becomes accustomed to crumbling or non-existent public services, with no opportunity to express their views or contribute to decision making.

But it is possible to tackle corruption, by creating strong and transparent institutions and encouraging an active civil society. In this, governments have a key role to play:

- ensuring free and independent media and judiciary;

- supporting parliaments which have the capacity to oversee policy;

- creating a meritocratic and effective civil service;

- fostering powerful audit institutions;

- institutionalising the participation of civil society and parliaments in making and implementing policy.

An important way of increasing government accountability to citizens is to provide free, universal access to basic public services. Once people recognise access to health and education services as their right, they start demanding effective delivery of those services. In Malawi, Uganda, and Ghana, pressure on the school system to improve its performance increased as parents came to know that they had a right to education for their children.[100]

There is a wealth of work by communities and civil-society organisations, often with the involvement of parliaments, across the developing world to expose corruption and improve government performance. The Concerned Citizens of Abra for Good Government (CCAGG), a Filipino citizens' group, has exposed several incidences of corruption in government projects, and its work has led to the arrest of culpable civil servants.[101] The Union for the Empowerment of Peasants and Workers in Rajasthan, India, demanded and obtained access to information which enabled poor people to secure the minimum wages that were their right. In the process a national campaign for freedom of information resulted in a new 'Right to Information' Law in 2000.[102] (Box 6 offers another example of success by civil-society groups in monitoring government performance.)

The way in which aid donors work with Southern governments is also pivotal in the fight against corruption. In recent years, donor aid has played a stronger role in prompting governments to improve their transparency and accountability. The IMF and World Bank have insisted on institutional reforms and measures to increase transparency – for example, requiring governments to make financial data publicly available.

Box 6: Follow the money – tracking education budgets in Malawi

Free primary education was introduced in Malawi in 1994 – but the Ministry of Education continued to be rocked by corruption scandals. When debt relief released new funds for the education sector, civil-society organisations were determined to see it well spent. Over the past three years, a national network of education organisations has worked closely with the parliamentary finance committee to monitor the spending of the money. They carry out annual nationwide surveys of primary schools, to see whether they are receiving basic resources such as basic as textbooks and chalk, as promised in the government budget. They also monitor the level of teachers' salaries and assess whether the government is meeting the targets for the numbers of new teachers trained. Their findings are widely reported in the media and used by parliament to demand greater efforts from government to ensure that the money reaches poor communities. The success of the initiative is clear: subsequent government reports have shown that the government did not transfer resources from those expenditures that were monitored.

(Source: Civil Society Coalition for Quality Basic Education [pers. comm.])

At the same time, however, some donors continue to withhold aid, reward a handful of 'good performers' (the approach adopted by the USA's Millennium Challenge Account), or channel it only through donor-managed projects. Such a strategy is in many cases counter-productive. It risks diverting money from where it is desperately needed. And it weakens the very government institutions that need support: donor projects, for example, may offer staff alternative employment for higher wages. In most cases, donors should invest in public institutions and government capacity; traditionally donors have funded capital projects, but have been reluctant to support recurrent expenditures such as salaries.

Even in the most difficult or conflict-affected environments, where states are unable or unwilling to promote poverty reduction, there are multiple ways in which to engage with poor populations. Aid can be deployed through a variety of institutions, of which civil-society organisations are a crucial element. State-led approaches such as the PRSP process can be adapted to the context, or introduced gradually. Adopting more flexible aid policies would enable donors to respond better to crises and, where necessary, to resume aid flows more quickly after crises have passed.[103]

The way in which aid donors work with Southern governments is also pivotal in the fight against corruption.

As Part 3 of this report has shown, aid tied to security and commercial imperatives also undermines efforts to tackle corruption. Rich-country donors must eliminate the global incentives for corrupt practice (see Box 7) and ensure coherence across development, diplomatic, and investment policies.

Box 7: Removing the global incentives to corruption

Corruption not only thrives in situations of weak domestic accountability, but is encouraged by poor international regulation of bribery, tax evasion, and money laundering — which often involves international business. Around the world there are at least 63 tax havens which enable multinational firms and developing-country elites to avoid their tax obligations, thus reducing the revenues for poor-country governments to invest in development. At a conservative estimate, the losses to developing countries from tax havens amount to at least $50 billion. Placing money in financial havens also allows corruption to flourish, because companies and individuals can hide the origins of their funds.

Donors must pay attention to private-sector governance as well as Southern government accountability, minimising tax avoidance by closing tax havens and defining common standards for multinational corporations; complying with the OECD's anti-bribery convention, which aims to detect, investigate, and prosecute bribery offences by international companies; and implementing the 'Publish What You Pay' initiative, requiring companies engaged in exploiting oil and natural resources to publish all payments that they make to governments.

(Source: Oxfam GB 2000)

Deliver policies and budgets for poor people, with poor people

For national governments to deliver development, they must also have policies in place which benefit the poorest. Pro-poor policies and budgets that allocate resources according to need are vital tools for ending poverty. The public budget is the most important tool for managing aid and redistributing resources. The main responsibility for this lies with national governments, but citizens can be a powerful force in demanding change on behalf of poor people, if the environment enables them to do so – and donors can help to create such an environment.

The voices and choices of poor people need to be included at every stage of the policy cycle.

The voices and choices of poor people need to be included at every stage of the policy cycle: from surveys which articulate their priorities, to consultations on the design of policy, access to information which enables citizens to scrutinise public spending, and monitoring of the impact on poor men and women. Laws in Bolivia in the 1990s institutionalised participation in policy making, and Vietnam likewise went through a complex process of consultation with its citizens when forming its five-year Social Economic Development Plan. The most well-known example is the Poverty Reduction Strategy Paper (PRSP) process. Although (as argued in Part 3 of this report), the PRSP process has its limitations, the approach has improved the poverty focus and consultation practices of many governments. In Ghana, the influence of civil society through the PRSP process has helped to focus attention on the more deprived areas in the north of the country.[104] In Zambia, the role of rapid agricultural liberalisation in exacerbating poverty was made clear by participatory research and by civil-society organisations during the PRSP process, leading to the government's decision to re-introduce support for some agricultural sectors.[105]

Devising pro-poor policies is a start – but the policies have to be implemented. That is what makes the budget so important. It is a government's clearest opportunity to demonstrate the sincerity of its commitments to finance improved health services, HIV/AIDS programmes, education reforms, water supplies, rural development, and income-generating opportunities. The publication of the budget is also the point at which the extent of donors' commitments to financing poverty reduction is clearly demonstrated. By determining who pays and who benefits from taxation, aid, and spending, the public budget can either reverse or compound poverty and inequality.

Many civil-society organisations well know the importance of the budget, and, around the world, they are engaging in extensive advocacy to improve budgetary processes. Some organisations track budget spending – as in Malawi; others analyse initial allocations to poverty reduction, and monitor who wins and who loses from public spending. 'Gender budgeting' assesses how the public budget will affect women and men differently, and investigates whether government policy is reducing inequalities in men's and women's access to resources (see Box 8). Poor women are often the biggest losers when the government fails to deliver adequate services. Their low social status and lack of financial resources means that they have

Box 8: Budgeting for equity: gender budgeting in Uganda

In Uganda, Oxfam and the Ugandan Forum for Women in Democracy (FOWODE) have been working together to analyse the impact of the government's agricultural extension programme on women subsistence farmers, who account for around 90 per cent of agricultural labourers. Although women are well targeted by the programme, those taking part in the Oxfam survey reported that they were unable to put into practice the agricultural advice that they received, because too little is being done to secure their land rights or provide suitable credit services. On the basis of the findings, FOWODE is discussing with government and parliamentarians how to improve the impact of the agricultural programme on the lives of women farmers.

(Source: FOWODE and Oxfam GB 2004)

Geoff Sayer/Oxfam

Uganda: women weeding sorghum near Moroto town, Karamoja

less access to private services when public services fail, but, given their traditional responsibilities for caring in the household, they tend to have the greatest need of public services.

Many governments are now directing a higher proportion of public spending to basic social services. A World Bank review of PRSPs in 14 countries shows an increase in poverty-reducing expenditure[106] of around 1.4 per cent of GDP over three years – comparable to a doubling of the health or education budget in most countries. And the share of poverty-reducing expenditure is set to rise rapidly in Africa, by two to five per cent of GDP across the continent.[107]

But there is plenty of room for improvement. Recent increases are still not great enough to offset the effects of harsh spending cuts during the era of structural adjustment.[108] The United Nations' 20/20 Initiative recommends developing-country governments to allocate at least 20 per cent of their public budget to basic social services – and recommends donors to do the same with their aid budgets. But most governments spend only around 13 per cent on such services,[109] and spending on health care and water supplies is particularly weak. Almost all countries in sub-Saharan Africa devote less than ten per cent of their budgets to health services – far short of commitments made in Abuja in 2001 to devote at least 15 per cent of their spending to improving health services.[110]

Box 9: Clearly not in the interests of poor people: abolish user fees for health care

'My wife died a few months ago. Very probably from malaria...but I don't know, since she never went to the health centre as we didn't have enough money. I don't even have enough to feed my two children, so how could I have paid the price of a consultation?'

Reverien, Bujumbura, Burundi *

The case for abolishing user fees for primary education is largely accepted, but fees continue to be charged for basic health care in most developing countries – and the effect on the poor is catastrophic.

By 1995, 28 out of 37 countries in Africa had introduced fees for basic health care. But infant mortality rose in Africa throughout the 1990s, while it was declining in Asia, Latin America, and the Middle East. The brunt of health-user fees is borne by the poorest in terms of high rates of mortality and disease, with millions unable to pay for even basic medical

consultations. In Ethiopia, where user fees have been in force for 50 years, the average poor person visits the doctor once every four years, and 80 per cent of households have at least one chronically sick person (Russell and Abdella 2002). Even small charges can force catastrophic financial trade-offs: the money often comes from the household food budget, or girls are taken out of school, or people sell their possessions or go into debt. When a price is put on access to health care, it is usually women and girls who pay.

Cost recovery does not make financial sense either, typically contributing less than 5 per cent to public health resources (Reddy and Vandermoortele 1996). As Uganda's success in abolishing user fees for health care shows, the measure can help a country to take great strides towards meeting the Millennium Goals, four of which are related to health.

* Cetinglu et al. 2004

Too often the largest share of public spending in developing countries goes to wealthy groups, who typically capture two to three times the share of health-care spending that benefits the poorest.[111] When governments introduce user fees for basic services, poor people are doubly squeezed. Charging people to use basic public services – a policy euphemistically known as 'cost sharing' in developing countries – is a tragic result of the under-funding and false 'efficiency' drives that were often prompted by structural-adjustment reforms in the late 1980s and early 1990s (see Box 9).

Donors have played their part in promoting the imposition of user fees. In 1998, 75 per cent of World Bank loans to sub-Saharan Africa included the establishment or expansion of user fees.[112]

Increasing resources is not enough on its own. Institutional reforms are also needed. In Uganda, improving the timing and management of budget releases to district health facilities was carried out in parallel with increases in the health budget. In Tanzania, education grants paid directly to schools have allowed school management committees to pay for what their schools need most.[113] To allow for effective public scrutiny of public policy, governments should improve the transparency of public information, legislating for public access to important documents. A survey of budget information available to citizens in five African countries showed growing demand from parliaments and civil society for better performance in public spending, but much room for improvement in the timeliness, accuracy, and availability of public information on budgets and spending.[114]

While developing-country governments can clearly do much to deliver better basic social services by increasing poverty-related spending and working well with civil society, the problem remains: poor countries lack the financial resources to achieve the MDGs. Recent case studies undertaken by Oxfam clearly show that the scarcity of financial resources is a key factor which weakens improvements in the way that institutions work. Lack of money leads to inefficiency, manifested in poorly paid staff and bad working conditions, deteriorating facilities, and a lack of proper equipment. Building classrooms without investing in basic equipment undermines the benefits of the initial investment.[115] And the financial resources required in the foreseeable future will have to be external. The cost of providing essential health interventions alone is estimated at between 10 and 15 per cent of GDP[116]– equivalent to the entire tax revenue in most Least Developed Countries.[117] Ultimately, the continuing lack of health care, education, clean water, and proper sanitation facilities for the world's poorest people is an international imperative – for which more and better aid is needed.

Tanzania: Noolosho Nakuta makes her case at a women's group meeting in Ngorongo District

Recommendations

In 2005, the G8 Summit, the UN Millennium Development Goals Special Summit, and the World Trade Organisation ministerial conference are unprecedented opportunities for action by donors and governments to end global poverty. For the world's poorest people, there is no time for empty rhetoric. To stand a chance of meeting the MDGs, in 2005 world governments must draw up a Millennium Plan which makes binding commitments to reform international trade rules, cancel the unsustainable debt owed by poor countries, and increase the volumes and effectiveness of aid. This must be followed by urgent and concerted action.

In relation to the debt and aid components of such a plan, Oxfam International makes the following recommendations.

All DAC donors are urged to take action as follows.

Increase finance for poverty reduction:

- Cancel 100 per cent of bilateral, World Bank, and African Development Bank debt owed by the poorest countries where relief is needed to enable them to reach the MDGs.

- Provide at least $50 billion in aid immediately, in addition to existing aid budgets, and set binding timetables in 2005 to ensure that all donor countries meet the target of allocating 0.7 per cent of their national income to aid by 2010.

- In addition to giving 0.7 per cent of national income in aid, support innovative mechanisms such as the IFF and international taxation to ensure immediate and sustainable development financing.

- Provide aid in the form of grants, not loans, where possible in the foreseeable future, and support the creation of an independent, fair, and transparent debt-arbitration panel to enable creditor and debtor countries to resolve debt crises without compromising poor countries' ability to finance vital social services, and without forcing them to repay what are considered by the panel to constitute odious debts. The use of export credits should be monitored by creditor governments to prevent the accumulation of unsustainable debts by developing-country governments.

- Contribute their equitable share to important global initiatives such as the Global Fund to Fight HIV/AIDS, TB, and Malaria, and the Fast Track Initiative.

- Provide long-term, predictable aid for investment in the provision of universal, free, and high-quality public services.

Make aid work best for poverty reduction:

- Fully implement Rome Declaration commitments to improve the delivery of aid and completely untie aid, including types of assistance omitted from DAC recommendations, namely food aid and Technical Assistance. The use and effectiveness of Technical Assistance spending should be the subject of a DAC review.

- Restrict the use of conditions to requirements for financial accountability and broadly agreed poverty-reduction and gender-equity goals only.

- Focus aid on the poorest countries and communities, enacting national legislation to mandate the use of aid solely for poverty-reduction purposes.

- Establish institutionalised and compulsory mechanisms to improve donor accountability for aid spending, such as independent monitoring groups and reviews by recipient governments.

- Link assessments of aid allocations to analyses of progress on poverty-reduction goals; such analyses should be broader than the macro-economic analysis currently conducted by the IMF.

- Actively promote an end to user fees for basic health and education services in all poor countries.

- Minimise tax avoidance by closing tax havens and defining common standards for multinational corporations; comply with the OECD anti-bribery convention; and ensure that the Publish What You Pay Initiative is implemented.

The World Bank and IMF are urged to take action as follows:

- Cancel 100 per cent of the debts owed to them by the poorest countries where relief is needed to enable them to meet the MDGs, revaluing IMF gold reserves and using the resources thereby generated to do so.

- Restrict the use of conditions to requirements for financial accountability measures and broadly agreed poverty-reduction and gender-equity goals only.

- Provide aid in the form of grants, not loans, where possible in the foreseeable future, on the basis of additional bilateral donor contributions to the World Bank's IDA facility. Support the creation of an independent, fair, and transparent debt-arbitration panel to enable creditor and debtor countries to resolve debt crises without compromising poor countries' ability to finance vital social services, and without forcing them to repay what are considered by the panel to constitute odious debts.

54 Low-income countries such as Angola, Kenya, and Nigeria, among the world's poorest countries (UNCTAD 2004), and countries, such as Ecuador, which, although middle-income, contain significant numbers of poor people and are adversely affected by debt crises.

55 For more details about the benefits of debt relief as a form of financing, see CAFOD, Christian Aid, and EURODAD 2003.

56 Switzerland cancelled all its bilateral debt, while Australia, Canada, Denmark, Italy, the UK, and the USA have made commitments to cancel their bilateral debts after HIPC countries have passed their 'Completion Point'. Austria, Belgium, France, Germany, Japan, and the Netherlands have promised to cancel all ODA-related debt before a certain cut-off date (UNCTAD 2004).

57 The proposal is limited to 14 HIPC countries and 18 other low-income countries judged by the UK government to be best able to use the debt money productively. These calculations follow the UK government's in calculating 'fair share' of the debt cancellation according to governments' contributions to the World Bank's IDA facility. The cancellation proposal includes the African Development Bank, because much of its debt cancellation is paid for out of the HIPC Trust Fund, or by bilateral contributions to the HIPC Initiative.

58 For a more detailed rebuttal of IMF and World Bank responses to cancellation proposals, see Kapoor 2003.

59 Even if all sub-Saharan African debt were written off, it would cover only half of the resource requirements for the region over the next decade (UNCTAD 2004).

60 Based on 2003 preliminary data. DAC donors account for around 95 per cent of global aid.

61 See Hogan 2004.

62 For more details, see the UK Treasury proposal at www.hm-treasury.gov.uk/media/1C7/AB/1C7ABBFE-BCDC-D4B3-115B84EA4BD07566.pdf

63 For more details on the Global Fund Against Hunger and Poverty, see Report of the Technical Group on Innovative Financing Mechanisms at www.diplomatie.gouv.fr/actual/pdf/Reportfieng.pdf

64 For other considerations raised by Oxfam relating to the proposals, see www.oxfam.org.uk/what_we_do/issues/debt_aid/downloads/globalfund_hunger.pdf.

65 Alesina and Dollar 1998.

66 The Development Assistance Committee (DAC) of the OECD defines which aid recipients belong in the ODA category and which in the second, known as Official Aid (OA) – see www.oecd.org/document/45/0,2340,en_2649_34447_2093101_1_1_1_1,00.html for details. Both must be provided by official government agencies, promote the economic development and welfare of developing countries, and be concessional in character, including a grant element of at least 25 per cent.

67 Japan has a clear policy of prioritising ODA to Asia, with some 57 per cent of bilateral ODA distributed to the region in 2002 (Oxfam Japan 2004).

68 Development Assistance Committee 2004 and Grimm 2004.

69 See Schifferes 2003 for details of pressure brought to bear on Angola, Guinea, and Cameroon, all non-permanent members of the Security Council; also Carroll 2003 and Africa Confidential 2003.

70 World Bank 2004a.

71 Details courtesy of the Global Economic Governance Programme, University College, University of Oxford.

72 UK bilateral spending in middle-income countries in 2004/05 and 2005/06 is to be reduced by around £100 million as a result (see http://news.bbc.co.uk/1/hi/uk_politics/3206379.stm). See also Reality of Aid 2004.

73 Tying also imposes other types of indirect cost, such as additional administration and the discouragement of donor co-ordination. See Jepma 1991.

74 See the Recommendation at www.oecd.org/dataoecd/14/56/1885476.pdf

75 See O'Connor 2003 and ActionAid 2004b.

76 And this figure is based on DAC statistics which include only 'project-related' Technical Co-operation. UNDP estimates are that when other types of Technical Co-operation are included, the real figure could be 10–20 per cent higher.

77 For a broader assessment of Technical Co-operation, see the analysis by Oxford Policy Management at www.opml.co.uk/docs/ACF5400.pdf.

78 A recent study found that the information content of commitments made by donors is either very small or statistically insignificant, with commitments overestimating aid levels, although due to donor pressure they continue to be used as the basis for budgetary accounting in recipient countries (Bulir and Hamann 2001).

79 See Monterrey consensus at www.un.org/esa/ffd/aconf198-11.pdf

80 See the declaration at
http://siteresources.worldbank.org/NEWS/Resources/Harm-RomeDeclaration2_25.pdf.
The indicators for measuring progress on the declaration can be found at
www.oecd.org/dataoecd/29/41/31661156.doc

81 The survey was undertaken in June–July 2004, with staff in various ministries in 11 developing countries, distributed evenly across regions. They were asked to express their opinions on various dimensions of donor practice by rating and commenting on donors with whom they had worked over the previous two years. Approximately 80 data points were generated for each donor, and donors for which there were not considered to be sufficient data were excluded from the final results. To encourage reliable responses, respondents' anonymity was assured at all times.

82 Bermejo 2004.

83 During the 1990s, the IMF imposed an increasing number of structural conditions. There has been no attempt to reduce macro-economic conditions, or those relating to governance and Public Expenditure Management, where the IMF is increasingly involved.

84 Killick 2004 and Eurodad 2003.

85 www.imf.org/external/np/exr/facts/conditio.htm

86 ActionAid 2004a.

87 See Oxfam International 2003.

88 See Oxfam International 2004.

89 ActionAid International 2004.

90 M. Lawson, pers comm.

91   Wilks and Lefrancois 2002.

92   Ministry of Finance and Economic Development, Uganda, 2002.

93   Deininger and Mpuga 2004; and Yates 2003.

94   The Suharto presidency in Indonesia ended in 1998; a general election followed in 1999. Bolivia's democratic transition arguably began with political reforms undertaken in 1985. Presidential elections in Nigeria in March 1999 led to civilian government after 15 years of military rule; Madagascar's democratic transition has been marked by progress and reversals, but was notable for the first transformation at the end of the 1980s and the removal of Admiral Ratsiraka from power in 1991. And in Kenya President Arap Moi's KANU party was defeated in multi-party elections in 2002. While such elections are not a guarantee of enlightened governance, they do nevertheless represent important milestones in the political history of these countries.

95   See Amoako 2004.

96   See http://emoglen.law.columbia.edu/CPC/archive/demotech/01FRIE.html for details about Ghana. For more details about the expansion of independent media in Africa, see Karikari 2004.

97   According to a recent poll by Transparency International (TI 2004).

98   *The Economist,* May 2004.

99   In Romania, the poorest third pay on average 11 per cent of their income in bribes, while the richest third pay just 2 per cent (World Bank 2004b).

100   Foster et al. 2002.

101   For details, see www.tag.org.ph/citizenaction/ccagg.htm

102   For details, see www.freedominfo.org/case/mkss/mkss.htm

103   For more detailed analysis of donor approaches in such situations, see Harmer and Macrae 2004 and Center for Global Development 2004.

104   Oxfam International 2002b.

105   Oxfam GB 2002.

106   The definition of poverty-reducing spending depends on the country, but usually includes primary education and basic health care, investments in rural development, and water and sanitation.

107   World Bank 2003b.

108   Zambia's per capita spend on health care fell by nearly 50 per cent in the 1980s and 1990s, for instance (Public World 2004, forthcoming).

109   UNESCO 1998.

110   For more details, see www.scienceinafrica.co.za/2004/january/aidsspending.htm

111   See Roberts 2003 and World Bank 2003b.

112   www.50years.org.

113   Although the system still needs improvement, and more than half of the grant destined for schools is retained by higher levels of government.

114 Folscher 2004.

115 Public World 2004, Report for Oxfam GB, forthcoming.

116 The Commission on Macroeconomics and Health estimates the cost of essential interventions at around $30 to $40 per capita, or around 10 per cent of GDP in least developed countries. A recent IMF study estimates the cost of meeting the MDG on infant mortality at 12 per cent of GDP (Musgrove and Zeramdini 2001).

117 The Commission on Macroeconomics and Health estimates the average tax take of low-income countries at 14 per cent of GDP (Musgrove and Zeramdini 2001).

References

ActionAid International (2004) 'Turning off the taps: Donor conditionality and water privatisation in Dar es Salaam, Tanzania', London: ActionAid.

ActionAid UK (2004a) 'Money Talks: How Aid Conditions Continue to Drive Utility Privatisation in Poor Countries', London: ActionAid UK.

ActionAid UK (2004b) 'Profile and Impact of DFID Technical Assistance', unpublished report, London: ActionAid UK.

ActionAid, CAFOD, and Oxfam International (2004) 'Fool's Gold: The Case for 100% Multilateral Debt Cancellation for the Poorest Countries', London: ActionAid, CAFOD, and Oxfam International.

Africa Confidential (2003) 'Special Report on Africa/Iraq and the United Nations Security Council', www.africa-confidential.com (last checked by the author October 2004).

African Development Bank (2002) 'Achieving the Millennium Development Goals in Africa: Progress, Prospects, and Policy Implications', African Development Bank.

Alesina, A. and D. Dollar (1998) 'Who Gives Foreign Aid to Whom and Why?', *NBER Working Paper* No.w6612.

Amjadi, A. and A. Yeats (1995) 'Have Transport Costs Contributed to the Relative Decline of Sub-Saharan African exports?', Washington: World Bank Policy Research Working Paper 1559.

Amoako, K. (2004) 'The capable state: a pillar of development in Africa', *New Economy* 11 (3): 132-7.

Bermejo, A. (2004) 'HIV/AIDS in Africa: international responses to the pandemic', *New Economy* 11 (3): 164-9.

Bhinda, N., J. Leape, M. Martin, and S. Griffith-Jones (1999) *Private Capital Flows to Africa: Perception and Reality*, The Hague: FONDAD.

Brautigam, D. (2000) 'Aid dependence and governance', Stockholm: Expert Group on Development Issues Working Paper 2000:1.

Bulir, A. and A. Hamann (2001) 'How Volatile and Unpredictable are Aid Flows and What are the Policy Implications?', Helsinki: WIDER.

Burnside, C. and D. Dollar (1997) 'Aid, Policies and Growth', Washington: World Bank Policy Research Working Paper 569252.

CAFOD, Christian Aid, and EURODAD (2003) 'Debt and the Millennium Development Goals', London: CAFOD, Christian Aid, and EURODAD.

Carroll, R., D. Campbell, J. Tuckman, and R. McCarthy (2003) 'The British do the diplomacy and the Americans write the cheques', *Guardian*, 28 February 2003.

Center for Global Development (2004) *On the Brink: Weak States and US National Security*, Washington: Center for Global Development.

Cetinoglu, D., P. Delchevalerie, V. Parqué, M. Philips, and M. Van Herp (2004) 'Burundi: Deprived of Access to Healthcare – Results of Three Epidemiological Surveys', Brussels: Médicins Sans Frontières.

CIA (2004) *The World Factbook 2004*, Washington: CIA.

Collier, P., L. Elliott, H. Hegre, A. Hoeffler, M. Reynal-Querol, and N. Sambanis (2003) *Breaking the Conflict Trap: Civil War and Development Policy*, Washington: World Bank and Oxford University Press.

Collier, P. and A. Hoeffler (2002) 'Aid, Policy and Growth in Post-Conflict Societies', Washington: World Bank Policy Research Working Paper 2902.

Congressional Budget Office (1997) 'The Role of Foreign Aid in Development', Washington: Congressional Budget Office.

Development Assistance Committee (DAC) (2004) *Development Cooperation 2003 Report*, Paris: OECD.

Dalgaard, C., H. Hansen, and F. Tarp (2002) 'On the Empirics of Foreign Aid and Growth', Nottingham: University of Nottingham CREDIT Research Paper 02/08.

Dehn, J. and P. Collier (2001) 'Aid, Shocks and Growth', Washington: World Bank Working Paper 2688.

Deininger, K. and P. Mpuga (2004) 'Economic and Welfare Effects of the Abolition of Health User Fees: Evidence from Uganda', Washington: World Bank Working Paper 3276.

Devarajan, S., M. Miller, and E. Swanson (2002) 'Goals for Development: History, Prospects and Costs', Washington: World Bank Working Paper 2819.

Dollar, D. and L. Pritchett (1998) *Assessing Aid: What Works, What Doesn't and Why*, New York: Oxford University Press.

Economic Commission for Africa (2003) *Economic Report on Africa 2003: Accelerating the Pace of Development*, Addis Ababa: Economic Commission for Africa.

EURODAD (2003) 'Streamlining of Structural Conditionality – What Has Happened?', Brussels: EURODAD.

Folscher, A. (2004) *Budget Transparency and Participation: Five African Case Studies*, Cape Town: IDASA.

Foster, M., A. Fozzard, F. Naschold, and T. Conway (2002) 'How, When and Why Does Poverty Get Budget Priority? Poverty Reduction Strategy and Public Expenditure Reform in Five African Countries', Overseas Development Institute working paper 168, London: ODI.

Global Campaign for Education (2004) 'Undervaluing Teachers: IMF Policies Squeeze Zambia's Education System', Brussels: Global Campaign for Education.

Greenhill, R. and S. Blackmore (2002) 'Relief Works: African Proposals for Debt Cancellation – And Why Debt Relief Works', London: Jubilee Research at the New Economics Foundation.

Grimm, S. (2004) 'European Development Cooperation to 2010: Aid Disbursement and Effectiveness', London: Overseas Development Institute.

Haggard, S. (1998) 'Graduating from Aid: Korea and Taiwan', Stockholm: Expert Group on Development Issues Working Paper 1998: 5.

Hansen, H. and F. Tarp (1999) 'Aid Effectiveness Disputed', Nottingham: University of Nottingham CREDIT Research Paper 99/10.

Harmer, A. and J. Macrae (2004) *Beyond the Continuum: The Changing Role of Aid Policy in Protracted Crises*, London: Overseas Development Institute.

Hertz, N. (2004) *I.O.U. The Debt Threat and Why We Must Defuse It*, London: Fourth Estate.

Hinchcliffe, K. (2003) 'The Impact of the HIPC Initiative on Education and Health Public Expenditures in African Countries', Draft: Human Development Department Africa Region.

HM Treasury (2002) 'Tackling Poverty: A Global New Deal: A Modern Marshall Plan for the Developing World', London: HM Treasury.

Hogan, M.J. (1997) 'Blueprint for Recovery', http://usinfo.state.gov/usa/infousa/facts/marshall/pam-toc.htm (last checked by the author October 2004).

International Institute for Strategic Studies (2003) *The Military Balance 2003–2004,* Oxford: Oxford University Press.

Intermón Oxfam (2004) *Realidad de la Ayuda 2004/2005,* Barcelona: Intermón Oxfam .

Jepma, C. (1991) 'The Tying of Aid', Paris: OECD.

Jolly, R. (2004) 'Global goals – the UN experience', *Journal of Human Development* 5 (1): 69-95.

Kapoor, S. (2003) 'Can the World Bank and IMF Cancel 100% of Poor Country Debts?', Dublin: Debt and Development Coalition Ireland.

Kapoor, S. (2004) 'The IMF, Gold Sales and Multilateral Debt Cancellation', Dublin: Debt and Development Coalition Ireland.

Karikari, K. (2004) 'Press freedom in Africa: challenges and opportunities', *New Economy* 11 (3): 184-6.

Killick, T. (2004) 'Politics, evidence and the new aid agenda', *Development Policy Review* 22 (1): 5-29.

Leipziger, D., M. Fay, Q. Wodon, and T. Yepes (2003) 'Achieving the Millennium Development Goals: The Role of Infrastructure', Washington: World Bank Working Paper 3163.

Lensink, R. and O. Morrissey (1999) 'Uncertainty of Aid Inflows and the Aid–Growth Relationship', Nottingham: University of Nottingham CREDIT Research Paper 99/3.

Lensink, R. and H. White (1999) 'Assessing Aid: A Manifesto for the 21st Century?', Stockholm: SIDA.

Ministry of Finance and Economic Development, Uganda (2002) 'Second Participatory Poverty Assessment Report', Kampala: Government of Uganda.

Musgrove, P. and R. Zeramdini (2001) 'A Summary Description of Health Financing in WHO Member States', Commission on Macroeconomics and Health working paper No. WG3. 3.

O'Connor, T. (2003) 'Australian aid: sustainable development for whom?', *Ethical Investor Magazine*, 10 January 2003.

Osei, R., O. Morrissey, and R. Lensink (2002) 'The Volatility of Capital Inflows: Measures and Trends for Developing Countries', Nottingham: University of Nottingham CREDIT Research Paper 02/20.

Oxfam GB (2000) 'Tax Havens: Releasing the Hidden Billions for Poverty Eradication', Oxford: Oxfam GB.

Oxfam GB (2002) 'Death on the Doorstep of the Summit', Oxford: Oxfam GB.

Oxfam International (2002a) *Rigged Rules and Double Standards: Trade, Globalisation, and the Fight Against Poverty*, Oxford: Oxfam International.

Oxfam International (2002b) 'Last Chance in Monterrey: Meeting the Challenge of Poverty Reduction', Oxford: Oxfam International.

Oxfam International (2003) 'The IMF and the Millennium Goals: Failing to Deliver for Low Income Countries', Oxford: Oxfam International.

Oxfam International (2004) 'From "Donorship" to Ownership: Moving Towards PRSP Round Two', Oxford: Oxfam International.

Oxfam International and Amnesty International (2003) *Shattered Lives: The Case for Tough International Arms Control,* Oxford: Oxfam International and Amnesty International.

Paton Walsh, N. (2003) 'US looks away as new ally tortures Islamists', *Guardian*, 26 May 2003.

Pogge, T. (2003) 'The First UN Millennium Development Goal', paper presented at the University of Oslo, 11 September 2003.

Public World (forthcoming, 2004) 'Delivering Good Quality Public Services: Health and Education', Oxford: report for Oxfam GB.

Reality of Aid (2004) The Reality of Aid 2004, Philippines: IBON.

Reddy, A., and J. Vandermoortele (1996) 'User Financing of Basic Social Services – A Review of the Theoretical Arguments and Empirical Evidence', New York: UNICEF Working Paper.

Roberts, J. (2003) 'Poverty Reduction Outcomes in Education and Health, Public Expenditure and Aid', Overseas Development Institute working paper 210; London: ODI.

Rodrik, D. (1994) 'Getting Interventions Right: How South Korea and Taiwan Grew Rich', NBER Working Paper 4964.

Russell, S. and K. Abdella (2002) 'Too Poor to be Sick – Coping with the Costs of Illness in East Hararghe, Ethiopia', London: Save the Children.

Schifferes, S. (2003) 'US lobbies smaller nations on Iraq', *BBC News Online,* 24 February 2003.

The Economist (2004) 'Georgia and Ajaria – the comic opera ends', *The Economist*, 6 May 2004.

Transparency International (2004) 'The Kenya Bribery Index', Nairobi: TI.

UNAIDS and WHO (2003) *AIDS Epidemic Update*, Geneva: UNAIDS.

UNDP (2004) *Human Development Report 2004*, New York: UNDP.

UNESCO (1998) 'Implementing the 20/20 Initiative – Achieving Universal Access to Basic Social Services', New York: UNESCO.

United Nations (2002) 'Technical Report of the High-Level Panel on Financing for Development', www.un.org/reports/financing/report_full.htm#4 (last checked by the author September 2004).

United Nations Conference on Trade and Development (UNCTAD) (2004) *Debt Sustainability: Oasis or Mirage?*, Geneva: UN.

United Nations Millennium Project (2004) 'Millennium Development Goals Needs Assessments: Country Case Studies of Bangladesh, Cambodia, Ghana, Tanzania and Uganda', www.unmillenniumproject.org/documents/mp_ccspaper_jan1704.pdf (last checked by the author September 2004).

Wilks, A. and F. Lefrancois (2002) 'Blinding with Science or Encouraging Debate?', www.brettonwoodsprojects.org/article.shtml?cmd[126]=x-126-15848 (last checked by the author October 2004).

World Bank (2002) *A Case For Aid: Building a Consensus for Development Assistance*, Washington: World Bank.

World Bank (2003a) 'Supporting Sound Policies with Adequate and Appropriate Financing', http://siteresources.worldbank.org/DEVCOMMINT/Resources/Fall-2003/DC2003-0016(E)-Financing.pdf (last checked by the author September 2004).

World Bank (2003b) *World Development Report 2004: Making Services Work for Poor People*, Washington: World Bank.

World Bank (2004a) *Global Development Finance: Harnessing Cyclical Gains for Development,* Washington: World Bank.

World Bank (2004b) 'HIPC Initiative: Status of Implementation', http://siteresources.worldbank.org/INTDEBTDEPT/PublicationsAndReports/20264190/HIPC-status-Of-Implem.pdf (last checked by the author September 2004).

World Bank and IMF (2004) 'Global Monitoring Report 2004 – Policies and Actions for Achieving the MDGs and Related Outcomes', Washington: World Bank and IMF.

Worldwatch Institute (2004) *State of the World 2004: The Consumer Society*, Washington: Worldwatch Institute.

Yates, R. (2003) 'Should African Governments Scrap User Fees For Health Services?', Kampala.

Background Research Reports

Arrizabalaga, I. and M. Arias (2004) 'Aid in the North: the case of Spain', Madrid: Oxfam Intermón (unpublished).

Calundungo, S. (2004) 'The Importance of International Aid in the Process of Post-war Rehabilitation in Mozambique', Madrid: Oxfam Intermón (unpublished).

Fraser, A. (2004a) 'Financing the Millennium Development Goals in Ethiopia', Oxford: Oxfam GB (unpublished).

Fraser, A. (2004b) 'Aid Relationships in Tanzania, with a Focus on Donors' Role in the Primary Education Development Plan', Oxford: Oxfam GB (unpublished).

Oxfam GB Survey of Donor Practices (2004) devised by A. Fraser and M. Lawson, Oxford: Oxfam GB (unpublished).

Oxfam GB and FOWODE (2004) 'Is Uganda's Plan for the Modernisation of Agriculture Benefiting Female Subsistence Farmers?', Oxford: Oxfam GB (unpublished).

Oxfam Japan (2004) 'Briefing Note on Japan's ODA', Tokyo: Oxfam Japan (unpublished).

Whiston, B. (2004) 'Decentralisation in Bolivia, Sierra Leone, and Indonesia', Oxford: Oxfam GB (forthcoming).